END

"We love because he first loved us."
(1 John 4:19)

The profundity of the Bible is epitomized in simplicity, for all the Law and the Prophets hang upon the precepts of loving God and loving people. The heart of the Christian faith is love because the heart of the Father is love. We were created in love, by love, and for love. It is only when we authentically connect to this God in intimacy that we are truly able to live out the Greatest Commandment.

The writers in this devotional have embarked on this beautiful journey of intimacy. They love well because they have allowed the Lord to love them well. As you read the following pages, receive the grace that is upon their words for you to encounter the Lover of your soul. This is a divine invitation to know Him more deeply than ever before. As you see His face and hear His voice, may you be transformed into His glorious image!

DAVID OH
Author of *Beginning in the Prophetic*
Overseer at the Southern California School
of Supernatural Ministry and Encounter LA

These brief but insightful reflections on Scripture focus on accessing the simplicity of faith often lost amid the apparent demands of religion. From the Martha and Mary story ("What's better than serving God? An intimacy with God when I receive from Him") to challenging the Prodigal Son's brother for not enjoying his father's blessing, each closes with several practical ways to respond—summarized in one memorable comment, "I can approach God anywhere and anytime as His child."

GORDON DALBEY
Author of *Religion vs. Reality: Facing the Home Front in Spiritual Warfare*

Throughout my life, I have encountered God in life-changing ways. I instantly connected to these devotionals. Each writer delves deep into personal and powerful encounters with God. Marked by supernatural love and transformation, these testimonies invite you to know God more intimately. I believe this book will launch you into deeper intimacy with God.

DR. CHÉ AHN
President and Founder, Harvest International
Founder, HRock Church
Pasadena, California
International Chancellor, Wagner University

Rholan's passion for intimacy with God is infectious and stirring. On reading this book you can't help but want more of the Lord and His presence in your life.

GER JONES
Senior Pastor, Vintage Church
Los Angeles, California

Rholan is a passionate and devoted worshiper of Jesus. His faithful joy in God's presence is always an encouragement to me.

BRENTON BROWN
Worship leader and Grammy-nominated artist

EXPERIENCING THE

SECRET PLACE

EXPERIENCING THE

SECRET PLACE

40 ENCOUNTERS WITH
THE HOLY SPIRIT

COMPILED *by* RHOLAN WONG

pronouns in Scripture that refer to the Father, Son, and Holy Spirit, and may differ from some publishers' styles. Take note that the name satan and related names are not capitalized. We choose not to acknowledge him, even to the point of violating grammatical rules.

DESTINY IMAGE® PUBLISHERS, INC.
P.O. Box 310, Shippensburg, PA 17257-0310
"Promoting Inspired Lives."

This book and all other Destiny Image and Destiny Image Fiction books are available at Christian bookstores and distributors worldwide.

Cover design by Eileen Rockwell
Interior design by Terry Clifton

For more information on foreign distributors, call 717-532-3040.
Reach us on the Internet: www.destinyimage.com.

ISBN 13 TP: 978-0-7684-5366-9
ISBN 13 eBook: 978-0-7684-5367-6
ISBN 13 HC: 978-0-7684-5369-0
ISBN 13 LP: 978-0-7684-5368-3

For Worldwide Distribution, Printed in the U.S.A.
1 2 3 4 5 6 7 8 / 24 23 22 21 20

CONTENTS

Introduction

HOW TO USE THIS BOOK

Experiencing the Secret Place: 40 Encounters with the Holy Spirit flows from the initial year of the Southern California School of Supernatural Ministry at HRock Church in Pasadena. Several of the staff and first-year students in the school were invited to share what they had learned about intimacy, and they submitted entries reflecting a wide variety of perspectives. Their forty entries in the book cover forty weeks of devotional readings. (Interestingly enough, the approximately nine months of that first school year equaled forty weeks of training.)

So, why forty weeks?

The number 40, as it marks lengths of time, seems to have a recurring significance in God's movement in history. God sent rain on the earth for forty days and nights, the Israelites wandered in the desert for forty years, Moses met with God for forty days and nights before receiving the Ten Commandments, and several of Israel's kings—including both David and Solomon—each reigned over Israel forty years.

Further, forty marks a length of time for progression into a new relationship with God and subsequent new responsibilities in the Kingdom. For example, Jesus was tempted in the desert for forty days before starting His earthly ministry, and His followers learned about the Kingdom of God for forty days before they started the first church.

I'd like to offer some practical suggestions as you read this devotional book.

Each entry is intended to be read and acted upon for a week. Use the full seven days, and resist the urge to prematurely skip to the next entry. Learning to live at a new level of intimacy with God means taking unhurried time to be with Him, so give yourself permission to luxuriate in each entry.

And even if certain entries appear initially inconsequential, I encourage you to follow through with them anyway. Each entry reflects a profound experience with God, with valuable perspectives and insights into intimacy. Whether you find a particular entry helpful or not, be assured that God desires intimacy so much with you that He will certainly meet with you during each week. You may find it beneficial to focus on each entry's "Next Steps" section and daily read and receive the "Blessing" written there for you.

Finally, I recommend enjoying, rather than analyzing, each devotional entry. The book is less a theological treatise and more an experiential guide. Give yourself the freedom to encounter God in new ways through these pages.

The staff and students at the school have experienced such peace and joy in their intimacy with God that they couldn't help but want to share what they have received. On behalf of all of them, I bless you over the next forty weeks with a deeper level of intimacy with God than you have ever known.

Let it be. Amen.

Rholan Wong

INTIMACY WITH GOD:
THE STARTING POINT

If you're reading this, please believe that it's not a coincidence that you picked up this book. God has planned for you to read this book and is calling you to a deeper relationship with Him.

How do I know this? Because God's heart is always seeking more intimacy with us.

So whether you've never talked with God and heard Him talk to you, or you have regular conversations with Him throughout each day, He wants even more intimacy with you.

At this point, you may be asking, "But where do I start?"

The first thing that many people who are beginning with God need to know is that He really wants to have a relationship with us. He's not apathetic; He passionately, desperately wants to know and be known by us.

Jesus tells us exactly how God views even those of us who have rejected Him. The tender, broken-hearted God laments, *"Jerusalem, Jerusalem, you who kill the prophets and stone those sent to you, how often I have longed to gather your children together, as a hen gathers her chicks under her wings, and you were not willing"* (Matt. 23:37).

Maybe the second thing to know is that, as the previous scripture tells us, our pasts don't make God angry at us or disqualify us from intimacy. We don't have to fix ourselves before God will accept us. He's not keeping a list of our sins and waiting for us to clean them up. The apostle Paul gives us the good news that *"God was reconciling the world to himself in Christ, not counting people's sins against them"* (2 Cor. 5:19).

In other words, sin is not the issue for God. Jesus paid for every sin we would ever commit, and God is therefore free to accept us just as we are. He's not angry with us, and we don't have to defend ourselves to Him.

So because God isn't holding our sins against us, we can have a new, open relationship with Him. We can, in Paul's words, be reconciled to God (see 2 Cor. 5:20-21).

If that sounds good to you, I would suggest that you're sensing a perhaps surprising truth—you already have a deep desire to be known by God and to know Him. The next step in your relationship with God can be just telling Him how you feel.

You might say something like this to Him:

God, I want a personal relationship with You. I want to hear You and know that You hear me. But I've kind of been going my own way and didn't realize that intimacy with You was even possible. Thank You so much that my past doesn't keep You from loving me. I say "yes" to Your call right now to an intimate relationship with You. Thank You for loving me as I start on this journey with You.

If you said that to God, you've taken the first step to more intimacy with Him. What a great time for you. I bless you with ever-increasing intimacy as you read this book.

Week 1

THE WHISPER MOMENTS

SCRIPTURE

The Lord said, "Go out and stand on the mountain in the presence of the Lord, for the Lord is about to pass by." Then a great and powerful wind tore the mountains apart and shattered the rocks before the Lord, but the Lord was not in the wind. After the wind there was an earthquake, but the Lord was not in the earthquake. After the earthquake came a fire, but the Lord was not in the fire. And after the fire came a gentle whisper. When Elijah heard it, he pulled his cloak over his face and went out and stood at the mouth of the cave. Then a voice said to him, "What are you doing here, Elijah?" (1 Kings 19:11-13)

COMMENT

I recently attended a college church campus service. I met a girl, young in age and in the faith, who asked me, "Why does it feel like intimacy with God is a one-way conversation?"

I totally understood her question and her desire to hear God. At the beginning of our journey into intimacy with God, we often begin a little confused and unsure of what to expect. In my journey I have come to learn the different ways He does talk to me. But I've realized I have sometimes missed His voice because I expected to hear Him in a big or even audible voice.

The prophet Elijah is overwhelmed by the attacks of the enemy. A queen has just declared a hunt for his life. He is terrified and running for his life.

Today we may feel the same way about areas in our lives that overwhelm us. We can even believe that the problem we are facing now will destroy our lives.

We cry, "Can someone please answer me? I'm so frustrated. The storm is here and I feel so alone."

Many times, our first response is to escape, to do what Elijah did—run to a cave and huddle down by ourselves. Or we seek solace in others by getting with our friends, going to church, or even making an appointment with the pastor.

I have come to learn that in the midst of any challenge, I will get the response I need in the whisper. I get on my knees and just wait for His peace and beauty to give me rest. The key to intimacy with God is not so much loud repetitive words but leaning on Him and resting on His chest.

I heard a pastor say that he asked, "God, why are You in the whisper?" The answer was powerful.

"Because that's how close I am to you."

Now, I'm not saying that He'll never use big and loud ways to get my attention. But intimacy requires trust and peace and knowing that He is always with me. I enter a deeper level of intimacy with God when I can abide from this truth: He is always close to me and is only a whisper away.

NEXT STEPS

1. Build a quiet place for you and God. It doesn't have to be much more than a spot on the floor in a closet, but dedicate this place to being alone with God.

2. Unplug the noise. In your quiet place, remove distractions, electronic and otherwise, and enjoy being silent before God.

BLESSING

Father God, I pray that right now we can breathe in this truth. May our hearts be filled with You and all You have for us. Whisper in our lives. May Your word transform our minds, our hearts, and our lives forever. We love You, and may we burn for You more every day. Amen!

—RUTH McGUIRE

"THE MOST NECESSARY THING"

SCRIPTURE

As Jesus and his disciples were on their way, he came to a village where a woman named Martha opened her home to him. She had a sister called Mary, who sat at the Lord's feet listening to what he said. But Martha was distracted by all the preparations that had to be made. She came to him and asked, "Lord, don't you care that my sister has left me to do the work by myself? Tell her to help me!" "Martha, Martha," the Lord answered, "you are worried and upset about many things, but few things are needed—or indeed only one. Mary has chosen what is better, and it will not be taken away from her" (Luke 10:38-42).

COMMENT

This familiar passage contrasts two ways of relating to Jesus. Martha wants to serve Jesus. But because she focuses on getting her home ready for His visit, she is anxious about the preparations and offended that her sister is sitting with Him and won't help her.

I think we can be a little hard on Martha. She had an admirable desire to give to Jesus. And, honestly, I'm often more like her than Mary. It's much easier for restless me to do something instead of just be with Jesus. And I'm not helped here by Christian leaders who, with good intentions, continually urge me to do more for God.

But Mary doesn't really care much about the social convention of hospitality or even about how much she can serve God. She's much too busy just listening to this One who loves her so much. She can't help herself; Jesus is just too captivating to resist.

What's better than serving God? An intimacy with God where I receive from Him.

I want to be more and more like Mary and be with Jesus. Rather than being so quick to give to Jesus, let me first receive from Him. I can be confident that Jesus loves me so much that He longs most of all to be with me and give to me.

Of course, this relationship will be the foundation of any service I offer. Jesus says, *"Freely you have received, freely give"* (Matt. 10:8). Once I have received from Him, I will have something to give.

NEXT STEPS

1. Are you naturally more a Martha or Mary? In other words, do you spend most of your

time on things to do for God or on receiving from Him?

2. Write down three ways you do rather than listen first.

3. Begin a regular quiet time with Jesus if you haven't already done so. This week, in your time with Jesus, invite Him to tell you what He wants you to know. Then just listen.

BLESSING

I bless you today with a heart to listen to Jesus. In the name of Jesus, I say no to a spirit of busyness and yes to the Holy Spirit of peace. Let it be. Amen and amen.

—RHOLAN WONG

ONLY ONE THING

SCRIPTURE

But the Lord said to her, "My dear Martha, you are worried and upset over all these details! There is only one thing worth being concerned about. Mary has discovered it, and it will not be taken away from her" (Luke 10:41-42 NLT).

COMMENT

Jesus tells Martha that there is really only one thing we should focus on—only one thing. It's just so like Jesus that He doesn't spell out what that one thing is. So what is this one thing? Well, we do know that Mary was sitting at Jesus' feet, totally consumed with Him.

I asked Jesus during my quiet time (just to make sure!), "What is the One Thing?" He said, "Me!"

When I started journaling with God, I was shocked when Jesus told me, "I am everything you need and you desire." I could only respond, "Surely not, Lord. I need to earn money, cultivate friendships, take care of my home."

But as we enter into His world, the world of the infinite, we learn that we can worship Him completely and then live out of the overflow of that worship. The rest of life becomes a byproduct or overflow of our focused intentionality on Jesus.

We learned two things from Mama Christeena Kale in the School of Supernatural Ministry. The first is that it is never a waste of time to spend time worshiping Jesus. And second, we should be intentional about that One Thing only; then we don't need to be intentional about anything else.

How can this be? It is as crazy as seeking the Kingdom first and having everything that the rest of the world is working for just given to us without self-effort (see Matt. 6:33). As we are intentional about seeking Jesus and worshiping Him, it seems that everything else in daily life gets done with ease and blessing as a side-effect or overflow. Hopeless relationships with years of no improvement change without effort. Frustrating or stressful tasks get accomplished with simplicity. We will look around and be amazed.

Receiving the desires of our hearts is a byproduct of our delight in and worship of our one true love. Remember Psalm 37:4: "*Delight yourself in Yahweh, and he will give you the desires of your heart*" (WEB). In fact, divine favor, knowledge of Kingdom secrets, and supernatural wisdom are all byproducts of the One Thing. God's promise is that when we seek Him with intentionality (all our heart) not only will we find Him, but He will give us things beyond our wildest dreams. How crazy and how cool is that?

NEXT STEPS

1. In your quiet time, ask Jesus to tell you what the One Thing is. We each need to hear and know this for ourselves.

2. For this week, put on hold every prayer request and all the things you have been contending for, and determine not to mention them to God. He knows your desires. Focus on Him. Focus on worshiping Him. Focus on blessing Him.

3. Get the Audiobooks app for your phone and download *The Practice of the Presence of God by Brother Lawrence.* (They are both free!) Close your eyes and listen—this is the writing of someone who gave his life over to worship every moment of the day in everything that he did.

4. This week, be intentional about the One Thing only. As you focus on worshiping Jesus this week, make a mental note of the byproducts in the rest of your life of such blessings as increased favor and ease in accomplishing things, improved personal relationships, and more fruit of the Spirit.

BLESSING

I bless you with a hunger and thirst to seek the One Thing. I bless you to sit at Jesus' feet and be intentional about seeking and worshiping Him. I bless you with the fulfillment of God's promise that when you seek Him with intentionality (all Your heart) you will find Him, and through Him additionally receive all things.

—GARLAND COHEN

TRUSTING IN THE SEASON OF THE UNKNOWN

SCRIPTURE

Trust in the Lord completely, and do not rely on your own opinions. With all your heart rely on him to guide you, and he will lead you in every decision you make. Become intimate with him in whatever you do, and he will lead you wherever you go (Proverbs 3:5-6 TPT).

COMMENT

In June of 2015, I was terminated from work due to a head-count reduction. Yet it was a season of my life when I was growing spiritually and confidently walking in the knowledge of who I am in the Lord and who He is in my life.

Although I knew in my heart that I trusted Him to direct my path, I didn't know if I was going to apply for another job or if He was going to use me in a full-time ministry.

Then in August of 2015, an acquaintance at my church offered me a job. She asked me to ask God if this job was His will. Fast-forward, I have now been doing the job for about nine months where I market the business to vendors. I love the job because it allows me to serve in four ministries that I love, babysit my granddaughter once a week on a weekday, and adjust my schedule whenever I want to.

I know in my heart that I am in His will. But because the job pays only commissions on signed contracts, it's now been almost two years without any significant income. We've spent the small savings that we had and most of our retirement funds.

I have dreams and visions of success that I hold close to my heart. Over and over again, I have received prophetic words that speak of prosperity and wealth. I've heard Him say in His still small voice, "I will bless you way bigger than what you can imagine."

I am in a season of an uncertain future, while I know in my heart that I fully trust Him. I will stand firm in whose I am and believe that He is greater than my situation. He is my God who loves me more than I can imagine, and I choose His purpose in my life. In this season, I have peace and uncontainable inner joy!

NEXT STEPS

1. In the time of the unknown, be intimately connected with Him. Read the Word! Allow Him to pour out His love over you and be open as He encounters you in your deepest need.

2. Don't let negative thoughts become big in your mind, or they will control you. The enemy wants to steal, kill, and destroy your confidence in the Lord. Speak and declare the living words of God into your life!

3. Be honest and open to tell God everything that is going on in your mind and feelings. He is faithful, and you can be confident that He will carry you to the next season of your life!

4. Don't put Him in a box by thinking how He should bless you. Trust Him to give you a greater blessing than you can imagine.

BLESSING

In your unknown season of life, I bless you with knowing that you are still growing spiritually. You can still hear Him speak to you, perhaps even in a clearer way because you are more open to Him. I bless you with hearing His unmistakable words to you and thus walking with Him more confidently toward the direction He is placing before you. I bless you with faith to believe that He is putting things in place behind the scenes for your greater good—in fact, even greater than what you can imagine. I bless you with a deep intimacy with Him and knowing that He is good. Finally, I bless you with faith in this season, a faith that would not lean on your own understanding, but would grow in this season of the unknown!

—RUTH KUIZON

Intimacy with God

Give unto the Lord the glory due to His name; worship the Lord in the beauty of holiness. (Psalm 29:2 NKJV).

"Well how do I start?"

First off, let's try just setting aside all previous methods, strategies, and styles of prayer for now. I have used a bunch of prayer books and intercession guides covering various topics to teach me how to pray for an hour or more, but at the end I felt I was just reading words off a page. I even tried my best at being "fervent" with kneeling, lying facedown, and standing. I tried using hand gestures and different voice inflections. But I finally decided that those behaviors just weren't me. Don't get me wrong. I did care about the situations and people I was praying for, but I just didn't feel very connected to God.

More than anything else, I wanted that heart-to-heart intimacy with God where He would share His secrets with me. But how could I do this?

Here is how: I started off my prayer time with twenty minutes of worship.

This non-negotiable discipline had to be developed. The first time I tried it, I ran out of things to say. I looked at my watch, and fewer than eight minutes had gone by. I had said all the "hallelujahs," "holy, holy, holys," "King of Kings," and "Lord of Lords" I could say. I realized I had used up all of my proper church words and was still not connected.

So I tried a different approach the next day. I did my eight minutes of church words, but I told myself I was going to sit there until the alarm went off to signal twenty minutes. Then a memory came to mind, and I started to thank God for getting me out of a recent bad situation. I started to describe some of His actions, such as, "Thank You, God, for keeping me safe that day." The idea of being safely kept stayed in my mind.

I started to speak naturally from my heart in such a surprisingly grateful tone that I was amazed. Some things I was saying were, "Lord, the way You arranged the other situation to keep me safe was amazing. You care for me so much that You kept me from making that wrong decision." Suddenly the alarm went off, and I realized that those last twelve minutes had passed by amazingly quickly and with such ease. I felt so connected with God and that all my needs were met, so I just got up and got ready for work.

I realized that, as I started with worship more and more and got better at it, there would be times that I did not have to make any requests. I knew that God knew what I needed and was dealing with that day.

One more story: I needed a financial breakthrough, and I brought it up during my twenty minutes of non-negotiable worship. But I felt bad about my request. So I said something like this: "Thank You, God, for providing the finances for me. You are amazing, and I know You love me and can do it again."

Yes, God says to ask for what I need, but at that point I put my needs higher than Him during this worship time. I didn't bring my finances up again during that prayer time. But when I was done with the twenty minutes, I just had a blessed assurance it was going to be taken care of. By that evening, everything had worked out and my needs were met. Amen!

NEXT STEPS

1. Try this week to start your quiet times with twenty minutes of worship. Determine in your heart that you will do this, no matter what. It will feel new and will take some time to get used to it, but once you realize how intimate those times can become, all the small stuff in your life will fade away.

Just make sure it is all about Him and His awesomeness.

2. Please don't feel like you have to limit yourself to twenty minutes. Go as long as you want until you feel you have made that connection. It will come. Just give yourself some time. Each time after that, it will get easier and easier, and the intimacy will be closer and stronger.

BLESSING

In Jesus' name, I bless your times of worship this week. Let joy fill you as you adore Him in the intimacy of your heart.

—STEVE PERKINS

DO YOU MIND IF I BLESS YOU?

SCRIPTURE

But he [the father] *said to him, Child, thou art ever with me, and all that is mine is thine* (Luke 15:31 DARBY).

COMMENT

These words were spoken by the father to his elder son in the parable of the prodigal son.

Most people who know this account focus on the younger son who wasted the money that his father freely gave him. Upon returning home, he was greeted lovingly and was fully restored to his place as a son. That could have been the end of the story except for the reaction by the elder son—a reaction I totally identify with.

My dad was a very frugal person, and I tried to earn his favor by not costing him very much money. For years, I would order the cheapest item on restaurant menus, which meant eating a lot of grilled cheese sandwiches. I was a good kid, like the elder son. (I even had the younger sister who got in trouble.)

The Lord used the loss of my favorite car to get my attention. I loved that car. It fit into any parking spot (definitely a plus here in Los Angeles) and needed very few repairs in its lifetime of 193,000 miles. So I just wanted that same car with fewer miles and no engine issues. God had a better plan.

While my husband and I were car shopping, I heard the Lord say, "Would it be alright if I bless you?" I believe most people would have no trouble responding quickly with a "yes," but this question took me by surprise. My heavenly Father was asking *my* permission to bless me, and it was my choice whether or not to receive His gift.

Like the elder son, I had been living with my Father while not really knowing His heart for me. The father's wealth had always been available to the son, but he had apparently never asked for anything. Instead of living with the privilege of being a son (who could certainly have thrown a party for his friends), he had lived as a servant.

Fortunately, I was able to say "yes" to His blessing. He provided me with a car that also fits into any parking space, has had very few repairs in over 200,000 miles, and—as a bonus—came with heated seats (a new experience for me). I am continuing to discover my privileges as His child and to recognize daily all His blessings.

NEXT STEPS

1. Do you relate to the elder brother in this parable? Can you recall a time when you were envious of someone else's life? Are you aware of your privileges as a son or daughter of your heavenly Father? Ask God to tell you about those privileges.

2. Are you familiar with the term "orphan spirit"? Simply put, it is not recognizing that when you ask for forgiveness for your sins through Jesus' death on the cross, you enter God's family as a beloved child. You are no longer an orphan but belong to Him. Unfortunately, you can continue to live life as an orphan unless you learn to act as a son or daughter. Allow the Father to show you if you do indeed have an orphan spirit and how it manifests itself through your choices. He wants to bless you, but He waits for your permission.

3. For your heart to embrace the truth of who you really are, you need to spend time in His presence. A couple of ideas: Listen to songs that speak of His great love for you. And find Scripture passages declaring you are His beloved. He desires to pull you on to His lap and share His life with you.

BLESSING

I bless you with the freedom and joy that come from knowing you are the Father's beloved child. "See how very much our Father loves us, for he calls us his children, and that is what we are!" (1 John 3:1 NLT)

—Linda Beeson

THE APPROACH

SCRIPTURE

Truly I tell you, unless you change and become like little children, you will never enter the kingdom of heaven. Therefore, whoever takes the lowly position of this child is the greatest in the kingdom of heaven (Matthew 18:3-4).

After Jesus and his disciples arrived in Capernaum, the collectors of the two-drachma temple tax came to Peter and asked, "Doesn't your teacher pay the temple tax?" "Yes, he does," he replied. When Peter came into the house, Jesus was the first to speak. "What do you think, Simon?" he asked. "From whom do the kings of the earth collect duty and taxes—from their own children or from others?" "From others," Peter answered. "Then the children are exempt," Jesus said to him. "But so that we may not cause offense, go to the lake and throw out your line. Take the first fish you catch; open its mouth and you will find a four-drachma coin.

Take it and give it to them for my tax and yours"
(Matthew 17:24-27).

*At that time the disciples came to Jesus and asked,
"Who, then, is the greatest in the kingdom of
heaven?" He called a little child to him, and placed
the child among them. And he said: "Truly I tell
you, unless you change and become like little children, you will never enter the kingdom of heaven.
Therefore, whoever takes the lowly position of this
child is the greatest in the kingdom of heaven.
And whoever welcomes one such child in my name
welcomes me" (Matthew 18:1-5).*

COMMENT

The first scripture reference tells us that our greatest identity is as His child. First and foremost, I am a son or
daughter of God. That revelation—and our understanding and acceptance of that high position—flows into
every part of our lives and is the foundation of all of our
being, thoughts, and actions.

On this side of the cross, it's easy sometimes to take
for granted that we are children of God. We know how
the story of Jesus ends. But back in biblical times, people
were just starting to experience Jesus and trying to make
sense of what He said and the miracles He performed.

It must have been so confusing to have the leaders in
the synagogue not see what they as lay people were seeing.
How could the heads of the faith be against the Messiah?
These fishermen were experiencing total acceptance from

Jesus and total skeptical criticism from the one place that defined their identity as Jews.

In the second scripture above, Jesus adds to the previous revelation that He is the Son of God by telling Peter that he, too, is a son of the King. They are brothers. To back up this astonishing idea, Jesus performs a miracle—supplying a temple tax for the sons, Jesus and Peter, from a fish that Peter catches. Jesus uses Peter's previous identity as a fisherman to reveal his superior identity as a son.

The implications of this divine identity may be lost on Peter, but the status is not. And he begins to verbally process this promotion to his peers. The disciples then come to Jesus to ask Him, "Who is the greatest in the Kingdom?" In other words, "Peter said he was a son like You. So what does that mean for the rest of us?" And Jesus gives us the clearest path to the presence of God the Father—being His child.

We can't take for granted the magnitude of the barriers this relationship removed for the Jews. Simply, very few Jewish men, and no Jewish women, could be in God's presence. Only one man, the High Priest, could approach the presence of God, and he could come only on special days. He had to undergo a rigorous ceremonial cleansing, and he had to bring sacrifices for himself and the people. He had to earn entry.

But at the cross, Jesus earned entry for each of us to approach God—not just to repent, but also to be close to Him like a child is with their father or mother. I can come to Him with a humility that says I have nothing to offer but my love and affection. Like a little child, I completely depend on my heavenly Father and experience the touch and comfort of knowing He is there.

God isn't looking for the clean, righteous, sacrificial, and ceremonial quiet time. He wants his baby boy or his baby girl to come and talk, to cuddle up, to process life together. I can approach God anywhere and anytime as His child. I don't have to bring anything or be anything. I can just be with Him.

NEXT STEPS

1. Let's thank Jesus right now for breaking the barriers and requirements for approaching God as our loving Parent. Take a moment if you need to ask Jesus to heal your heart from the wounds that your earthly father or mother created by being unapproachable. Ask Holy Spirit to guide you to God as the Father and Mother, and allow yourself to just sit in the presence of a loving Parent.

2. What barriers or qualifiers have you inadvertently put up that limit when you talk to God? Can you only talk to God during "quiet time"? Must you repent and feel clean before you can talk to God? Did you know you could talk to Him all day or any part of the day? Whenever you wish and no matter what else is happening?

3. If you have had a good relationship with your parents, think of the reasons and ways that you talk to them. Sometimes there is no obvious reason to be with them; you just want to check in. And don't limit God to just being a dad! We approach dads and moms for different things and in different ways. God is Dad and Mom to us, so we can approach God either way. And if you have children of your own, think about your response when they call or want to talk. Our kids don't need a reason to come to us. We love them and enjoy every second they desire to talk and let us into what they are thinking.

    Talk to God right now in a way you have never spoken before. Approach Him as Dad or approach Him as Mom. Approach without a problem, but instead with some good news! Or approach Him with your confusion or process. There are no boundaries to how we can approach God.

4. Practice approaching God differently this week. For example, when your identity is challenged, remind yourself of an unchanging truth—you are a child of God. You might ask Him what He thinks of His precious son or daughter.

BLESSING

I bless you to know and believe that you are a child of God—your greatest and eternal identity. With that identity comes great privilege and reward. Peace and joy are yours, my brother and sister. I bless you to approach God as Daddy and Mommy and grow in the intimacy of that truth.

—Tenessa Audette

MEETING ONE ON ONE

SCRIPTURE

Jesus entered Jericho and was passing through. A man was there by the name of Zacchaeus; he was a chief tax collector and was wealthy. He wanted to see who Jesus was, but because he was short he could not see over the crowd. So he ran ahead and climbed a sycamore-fig tree to see him, since Jesus was coming that way. When Jesus reached the spot, he looked up and said to him, "Zacchaeus, come down immediately. I must stay at your house today." So he came down at once and welcomed him gladly. All the people saw this and began to mutter, "He has gone to be the guest of a sinner" (Luke 19:1-7).

COMMENT

I sometimes catch myself thinking that the odds of God showing up increase when more people are around. Sunday church services, for example, are more likely to see God revealing Himself than weekday small-group meetings. And the crusade, the conference, and the concert will surely see more of God's presence.

But as good as all those group meetings are, Jesus seemed to have a different view. Instead of choosing to speak to a large crowd, He points to a single man whom He will be with.

Why would He make such a choice?

Maybe because He longs so much for intimacy, Jesus will often choose a single person rather than a crowd. He knows I can be more intimate with Him in my quiet time than I would be in a crowd of people.

Jesus never ignores the one in favor of the many. There is no such thing as being lost in the crowd where Jesus is concerned. He looks beyond the crowd to see and choose each one.

NEXT STEPS

1. List some of the advantages and disadvantages of meeting God in large groups and being alone with Jesus.

2. Do you think that the larger the group, the more likely Jesus will show up? Or do you look for Jesus in larger gatherings? Or maybe even wait to call on Him until you're with others?

3. In your devotional time this week, start by thanking Jesus that He wants to be with just you. He's not looking around hoping that this time with you will end so that He can

meet with a larger group of people. He is looking forward to being with you.

BLESSING

In the name of Jesus, I bless you with the revelation that He has chosen to be with you this week. May your heart open up to the One who desires you more than a crowd.

—Rholan Wong

THE GRACE OF GOD

SCRIPTURE

The incomparable riches of his grace, expressed in his kindness to us in Christ Jesus (Ephesians 2:7).

COMMENT

I grew up in church and never understood what grace really was. That's because I never heard about grace the way Paul intended us to understand it. I heard the Gospel and knew how to pray, but I still only understood a portion of what grace is. It wasn't until my second year of Bible college when I understood what grace really was, and everything changed!

Let me give you an analogy. Imagine you were speeding. Now you were not accidentally speeding but intentionally, guilty-as-charged speeding. You may even have had a great time doing it! But you got caught, you knew it was wrong, and the law has to take over. The police officer comes up to you and says, "Look. I caught you going 25 miles per hour over the speed limit. This is a clear violation of the law, and for that you need to be punished. But, because I am officer for the law, I can let you go. Just don't do it again."

Now that seems like a great deal. Who wouldn't want that! I know I would. In my previous understanding, I would say this is grace. And if you think this way, you are not wrong. But even this illustration is still limiting grace. This is a clear example of mercy, but not of grace. Grace is even more.

The officer comes up to you right after you've committed the crime, looks you up and down, and says, "I know you know this was wrong. But instead of giving you a three-hundred-dollar fine, I am going to give you three hundred dollars. And I would also love to invite you over to dinner. You can bring your family and anyone else you wish. You are now my friend; and as my friend, I want to introduce you to my colleagues to show them what an outstanding citizen you are!"

Wow! Now that is grace! Did you spot the difference? The first example is a display of mercy, a reprieve from punishment. The second example is a display of grace—a gift of unmerited, undeserved favor.

Do you know that God did not just stop with mercy, but He gave you grace as well? *Simply put, the grace of God is the supply of everything that Christ has done and finished on the cross! Brothers and sisters, that is good news. God did not just stop with a pardon, but He gave us a powerful exchange!* Like the officer in the illustration, He went beyond mercy and gave you a supply, invited you into His family, and displayed you as righteous even though you didn't deserve it.

Let's take a look at what God has freely given us.

- Forgiveness of sin: Ephesians 1:7
- Purchase of our healing: 1 Peter 2:24
- Adoption as His children: Romans 8:15
- Righteousness because He became sin for us: 2 Corinthians 5:21
- Freedom from condemnation: Romans 8:1
- Birth as a new creation: 2 Corinthians 5:17
- His Holy Spirit: Ephesians 1:13
- Every spiritual blessing: Ephesians 1:3
- Divine authority: Matthew 28:18-19
- Oneness with Him: 1 Corinthians 6:17

Want more great news? *Most of the promises mentioned in the New Testament are grace based!* They are not conditional on your performance but on Jesus' sacrifice. They will forever be yours because of God's undeserved, unmerited favor. They are a gift, not a reward. We have gone from a Covenant of Old that was dependent on us to a Covenant of New that is dependent on Jesus. This is truly passing from glory to glory (see 2 Cor. 3:18).

NEXT STEPS

1. Read all the verses mentioned. Ponder them until you understand more of how beautiful Christ is.

2. Dive into some teachings of grace from the New Covenant perspective. You might study the eighth, ninth, and tenth chapters of Hebrews.

3. Instead of asking God for forgiveness or righteousness, thank God that His one sacrifice purified you for all eternity.

4. Begin and end your prayer and worship with thanksgiving.

BLESSING

In Jesus' name, I bless you with a deep intimacy with God as you live in the grace that He offers you. Amen.

—ANTHONY TUSSING

SURRENDERING IN THE WILDERNESS

SCRIPTURE

My fellow believers, when it seems as though you are facing nothing but difficulties see it as an invaluable opportunity to experience the greatest joy that you can! For you know that when your faith is tested it stirs up power within you to endure all things. And then as your endurance grows even stronger it will release perfection into every part of your being until there is nothing missing and nothing lacking (James 1:2-4 TPT).

COMMENT

This past year has been one of those years when I felt like I was trudging through mud with no way out. I experienced one of the greatest heartbreaks of my life, and it happened in the church. To be honest, I think it almost broke me. I had put my leaders on a pedestal that they did not belong on, and when the devastation came I went into a time when I really wanted nothing to do with the church. Even when I did go to church, I hid in the background, not wanting to be known.

I learned the hard lesson that putting people instead of Jesus on a pedestal usually means disillusionment. Unfortunately, my story is all too common, and too many Christians end up leaving their churches. I had to remember that even leaders in the church can let me down. But I can choose to keep my eyes on Jesus so that when I face inevitable disappointment, trials, and tribulations I will persevere until I come out on the other side rejoicing and having greater faith in my life.

NEXT STEPS

1. Take a moment and ask Holy Spirit if you have placed anyone on a pedestal who does not belong there. If He reveals anyone to you, ask for forgiveness and ask Jesus to take His throne again in your life.

2. Ask Holy Spirit if there is anyone you need to forgive to prevent bitterness from lingering in your heart. Forgive and bless them. Surrender your need to understand or have retribution for the hurt you have faced. Ask Jesus to come and heal your heart so you can move forward.

3. Find someone you can be vulnerable with to share how you are feeling. It is good to find a safe person to process with, someone who

won't be afraid to call you out when you need to be corrected. Ask them to be praying for you during your trial or tribulation.

BLESSING

Jesus, I thank You that You are the King on the throne who watches over us. I thank You that You are perfect love and in You there are no faults. I pray for everyone reading this who has been hurt by the church. Come and walk them through their healing. Bring reconciliation and restoration to Your people and the church that You love so much. Help us to remember that You are on the throne and no one else. In Your beautifully wonderful name, amen.

—MINDY RIVAS

PROVISION THROUGH INTIMACY

SCRIPTURE

Now Elijah the Tishbite, from Tishbe in Gilead, said to Ahab, "As the Lord, the God of Israel, lives, whom I serve, there will be neither dew nor rain in the next few years except at my word." Then the word of the Lord came to Elijah: "Leave here, turn eastward and hide in the Kerith Ravine, east of the Jordan. You will drink from the brook, and I have directed the ravens to supply you with food there." So he did what the Lord had told him. He went to the Kerith Ravine, east of the Jordan, and stayed there. The ravens brought him bread and meat in the morning and bread and meat in the evening, and he drank from the brook. Some time later the brook dried up because there had been no rain in the land. Then the word of the Lord came to him: "Go at once to Zarephath in the region of Sidon and stay there. I have directed a widow there to supply you with food." So he went to Zare-phath. When he came to the town gate, a widow was there gathering sticks. He called to her and asked, "Would you bring me a little water in a jar so I may have a drink?" As she was going to get it, he called, "And bring me, please, a piece of bread." "As surely as the Lord your God lives," she replied, "I don't have any bread—only a handful of flour in a jar and a little olive oil in a jug. I am gathering a few sticks to take home and make a meal for myself and my son, that we may eat it—and die." Elijah said to her, "Don't be afraid. Go home and do as you have said. But first make a small loaf of bread for me from what you have and bring it to me, and then make something for yourself and your son. For this is what the Lord, the God of Israel, says: 'The jar of flour will not be used up and the jug of oil will not run dry until the day the Lord sends rain on the land.'" She went away and did as Elijah had told her. So there was food every day for Elijah and for the woman and her family. For the jar of flour was not used up and the jug of oil did not run dry, in keeping with the word of the Lord spoken by Elijah (1 Kings 17:1-16).

COMMENT

I have felt closest to my heavenly Father when I've seen Him do for me what I could never do. Yes, miracles are amazing. But if I don't realize that a miracle proves God's love for me, I risk being like those who perform miracles in His name but are never known by Him (see Matt. 7:22-23). If miracles don't lead me to love Him more, go deeper in my understanding, and surrender to His ways, then I've missed the heart of the supernatural.

So, what do I need more of? What do I find myself in a shortage of today? Have I let myself believe that God isn't willing or able to provide for me in the area I am seeking more in?

Elijah certainly struggled with these kinds of questions. He had faithfully done exactly what God had asked of him, but he still found himself in very discouraging circumstances. And he knew that he couldn't do anything to change the situation without God's help.

Through Elijah's experience with the drought, I learn God wants to show me that He's able to turn the little I have into a lot! This miracle of provision, the account of Jesus multiplying the two fish and the five loaves (see Luke 9:12-17), and many other biblical passages show me that God can indeed meet my impossible need.

For me, making this truth real comes only when I choose to sit quietly with Him and reflect on who He is and what He has done. I have to focus solely on Him so that my circumstances don't influence how I think about a situation. Then, I can hold to the core truth that He is still doing what only He can do—and doing it all of the time because in all things He is at work for my good (see Rom. 8:28).

God always has a good solution when I am in serious need. Seeking the solution can either draw me closer to Him or it can create distance and offense if I don't see what I want to see when I want to see it. God told Elijah to walk ninety miles through the desert during one of the region's greatest droughts while being pursued by King Ahab's mighty army. But Elijah then found God's solution to his need—abundant provision through a most unexpected source of a poor widow who thought that her life was over.

NEXT STEPS

1. Do you keep track of your personal history with God? I recommend keeping a record so you can remember what God has done in your life that you could never do on your own. In our first year at the School of Supernatural Ministry, Ali and Kyle Gattison shared that they had prayed and declared that Ali's allergic skin condition would be cleared up, and God healed it! I was so moved by this that I asked them to pray for my amazing wife, Beth. Beth had the worst dairy and milk product allergies that I'd ever seen. If she ate any kind of dairy product, she'd have hives all over her body for three or more months. I often had to ice her down before she'd go to work to alleviate her discomfort. After Kyle and Ali prayed for her, God healed her and our lives were radically changed forever. Whenever I consider if God can heal someone or do

a miracle, I remember my personal history with Him and my faith is always renewed!

2. Is there a time in the past when God gave you either a different answer than you wanted or you felt that He didn't answer at all? Have you allowed a spirit of offense to turn you away from trusting God as the One who can provide for you? Is there something in your relationship with Jesus that needs to be dealt with? If so, consider going to your secret place with Jesus and opening your heart to Him. You may want to take time, as David did in the Psalms, to complain, argue, and ask God to speak to you about that situation.

3. Press on in sharing God's Kingdom! Often times when I feel that I'm in deep need or that I can't see how God can provide, I'm tempted to pull away from my calling to continue advancing the Kingdom. If you aren't feeling good about where you're at, I would encourage you to love and pray for others in spite of how you're feeling. Be encouraged by what God can do through you and in your life in any circumstance when you allow Him an opportunity.

BLESSING

I bless you with faith to trust that God can do anything in any circumstance! A faith that has eyes to see what He is doing and to stay faithful in your circumstances until God shows you the answer for your need through intimacy with Him! For His glory! Amen.

—ZAC KINTNER

A GIFT FOR THE KING

SCRIPTURE

So shall my word be that goeth forth out of my mouth: It shall not return unto me void, but it shall accomplish that which I please, and it shall prosper in the thing whereto I sent it (Isaiah 55:11 KJV).

For we are fellow workmen (joint promoters, laborers together) with and for God (1 Corinthians 3:9 AMPC).

Laboring together [as God's fellow workers] with Him (2 Corinthians 6:1 AMPC).

COMMENT

This is the day we've all be waiting for—when the King allows His subjects into His throne room. So much pomp and circumstance! I may be only a page, an attendant, in the palace of the King of Kings, but I get to go into the room, too, and bring my gift to Him.

When the King welcomed me into the palace some years before, He gave me a gold crown that was much too big for my head. It is still a bit wobbly on my head, but fitting better.

My gift is this crown, my most prized possession. I've added some precious stones to the crown and put it on a pillow of the most expensive silk in the royal colors of purple and gold.

I'm so excited, grateful, and overwhelmed to be in the King's presence. I've longed to bring to the King something of value to express my heartfelt emotions for the kindness He extended when He rescued me from my former life of poverty, brokenness, and disease.

The distance from the entryway up to the King's throne is quite lengthy, but I'm determined to walk it in the most dignified manner due the King. I take measured steps, hold my head high, and extend my hands to lay the crown at the King's feet.

There He is. I kneel down, placing the crown and pillow at the King's feet. Now that I am so close to Him, I have to lie prostrate and call out words describing this Man's goodness, purity, and so much more! I can't say how much I owe him.

Suddenly, I hear the King calling my name in a commanding tone. Oh, no! What have I done wrong? I thought He would be pleased with my gift.

Again the King calls my name and says, "Page, *stand up!* Come closer."

He tells me that now is not the time to worship Him or to serve within the palace.

"Come closer, bring your crown with you, let me place it upon your head," He says. "Come sit on this throne to my right. You are to rule and reign over all with Me! This will be your time of preparation, and I shall be your teacher. You will learn of your Kingdom and its peoples, your authority and the emblems of that authority such as the scepter and royal rings, your allies and enemies, and the protocols of a royal ruler."

As I look back on that day, I remember that instruction began immediately. As the King received visitors, there was so much to remember. I learned not to differentiate between the poor and wealthy when administering their affairs and to listen carefully and intently to our enemies as well as our allies. I even learned the proper posture and speech of royalty.

When I first came to the palace, the King told me that one day we would reign together in His Kingdom. I did not believe Him; I thought He was just being kind to make me feel comfortable in His presence. Besides, I had never heard of a worthless pauper ruling with the King.

Today, I see differently. I understand that the King's words are full of authority and power. His words are not vain, and what He decrees comes to pass. And He has said He *does* want me sitting here at His side ruling with Him! I will accept that and walk in my new position.

NEXT STEPS

1. How many of us can join with the page saying that we, too, have been guilty of not believing what Jesus has said to us? There's no condemnation here, but a call to faith. Ask Holy Spirit to remind you of the many promises spoken to you about, for example, your destiny. Or recall something Jesus has promised you and decide to believe Him, whether you see it now or not.

2. Are we ready to be prepared? Will we pick up our crown and let Him place it on our heads, submitting to our King's training as He transforms us into a co-laborer with Him?

3. Spend some time alone this week with Jesus. Tell Him that you accept His call to rule with Him and ask Him what the next step is in your training.

BLESSING

In Jesus' name, I bless you with intimacy as you hear God tell you His plans for you and your destiny to rule with Him.

—SHERYL BEACON

BEING JESUS' BELOVED BRIDE

SCRIPTURE

Blow upon my life until I am fully yours. ...Come taste the fruits of your life in me (Song of Songs 4:16 TPT).

I've made up my mind. Until the darkness disappears and the dawn has fully come, in spite of shadows and fears, I will go to the mountaintop with you—the mountain of suffering love and the hill of burning incense. Yes, I will be your bride (Song of Songs 4:6 TPT).

COMMENT

What a radical prayer! A prayer with such meaning that I shouldn't pray it if I don't mean it.

Even so, this prayer was and still is the cry of my heart. I didn't know what life would look like on the other side of that prayer, but I counted the cost and found it was worth all I had and all I was in order to have Jesus make me His bride. The other side of that prayer has been a great adventure of ups and downs, as all of life is, but with a new focus—Jesus and His passionate love for me.

Being His bride shifted my entire worldview as I couldn't stop thinking about this one thing—Jesus wants *me* for His bride! He isn't satisfied with me remaining His servant or His friend or even His king and priest.

He wants to be my everything and He wants me to be His everything. His heart is for intimacy. He says, *"I am undone by your love"* and *"You have stolen my heart"* (Song 4:9 TPT). Wow! I have stolen the heart of the King of Kings!

He alone is my Beloved and I want no one else. I still pray, "Come walk into me until I am fully Yours. Come taste the fruits of Your life in me." We, my Beloved and I, have started our exciting journey together of becoming one, and I am daily glad He answered the cry of my heart.

NEXT STEPS

1. Do you long for more intimacy with Jesus? Can you believe He longs for more intimacy with you? Or are "shadows and fears" holding you back? Perhaps it is time to say "yes" to His invitation to be His bride. You can make this your prayer: "I've made up my mind. Yes, I will be Your bride."

2. Husbands and wives joyfully look forward to time they can spend with each other. In your devotional times this week, invite Jesus

to tell you how He loves you, and tell Him why you love Him.

3. Husbands and wives also openly share whatever is on their hearts. In your time with Jesus this week, tell Him what you are thinking, no matter how inappropriate you may think it is. And then invite Him to tell you whatever He wants to.

BLESSING

May each day the fruits of your life taste sweet to your Bridegroom King, Jesus, as He draws you ever closer to His heart.

—Judi Peterson

ABIDING IN JESUS

SCRIPTURE

Abide in Me, and I in you (John 15:4 NKJV).

COMMENT

Sounds simple doesn't it? Yet at times, my definition of "abiding" gets subtly layered with nuances that bury the original meaning of staying in such a close relationship with Jesus that it may be said we are in each other. We are inseparable. But if I am not careful, I may miss the simplicity of abiding in Him.

So what is abiding not like?

Abiding in Jesus is not adding a layer of routine that leads to ritual.

And it's not a layer of effort that can lead to work.

And it's not even a layer of rest that can lead to laziness.

If I add any of these things to abiding, I have deceived myself into creating a new definition of "abide."

So what is abiding?

Abiding is guarding the time I have with Jesus.

Abiding is hearing the voice of the Holy Spirit in my spirit and resonating with Him.

Abiding is pursuing the loving heart of my Abba Father.

And the same can be said in reverse! Jesus guards the time He has with me. Holy Spirit is hearing my voice and resonating with me. Abba is pursuing my heart of love.

This is the most intimate relationship I have because the Creator God of the universe has made me His home. I am the Ark of the Covenant—in me He lives! And I live in the heart of the Father.

NEXT STEPS

1. In what ways have you added to the meaning of abiding in Jesus?
2. What does abiding in Jesus mean to you? How can you abide in Him?
3. In your devotional time this week, focus on just being with Jesus. Try to come to your time with an open mind and no agenda other than just being with Him.

BLESSING

In the name of Jesus, I bless you with a hunger to be with Jesus. At any and all times of your days this week, may you abide in Jesus as He abides with you. Selah.

—Jenney Oh

TURNING YOUR GAZE UPON HIM

SCRIPTURE

Here's the one thing I crave from God, the one thing I seek above all else: I want the privilege of living with him every moment in his house, finding the sweet loveliness of his face; filled with awe, delighting in his glory and grace. I want to live my life so close to him that he takes pleasure in my every prayer (Psalm 27:4 TPT).

COMMENT

All it takes sometimes is a moment to tune in to the Lord and His love for you. And that moment can change everything!

In the past I once had lots of time, hours upon hours while my kids were in school, to lavish on Him in intimate worship and communion. That was a wonderful season that I will always cherish in my heart, because these days I have less time to just sit at His feet. But even though I can often only spend minutes instead of hours, my communion is still deep and direct. He is as close as the air I breathe. There is no distance as I turn my gaze toward Him. He is still brilliant and glorious, and I am still enraptured by His beauty and awed by His humble and unconditional love.

I realize there is no formula for intimacy. I used to say that I needed to spend a lot of time with Him to develop intimacy. Like the Shulamite in the Song of Songs under the apple tree, to be undisturbed as I rested in His embrace is such a delight that I never wanted that time to end. What a grace to have undisturbed time to just be with Him, to rest in Him, to look at Him, and to hear Him call me His beloved. That season of deep intimacy in rest got me through one of the most difficult times in my life.

But I also understand now that intimacy with God is not about the quantity of time (although what a gift that grace is during those seasons). It is about the heart that yearns for, hungers for, searches for, surrenders to, and finds the One who is Love. Sometimes those little moments of remembering, focusing, looking, and receiving in the midst of the busyness of life allow us to stay and abide with Him throughout the day.

And here is another revelation: intimacy isn't about my strength to *do* something (like spend a bunch of time), but just a surrender to His strength to *be* fully His! To be loved! And to be led by His Spirit into deeper encounters in worship.

NEXT STEPS

1. Carve out some time each day this week to be with God. Don't skip this time, even if it is short. Then allow yourself to be gently led by His gracious Spirit into a time of intimacy that your heart is longing for. Tune and turn your heart in those moments to Him. He will satisfy!

2. Remember a past time when you felt those quiet nudges from the Holy Spirit. Ask God to help you the next time you feel these nudges to pause, turn the eyes of your heart to Him, and tune in to His love for you.

3. Be especially sensitive to short times during the day when you can turn your heart toward God. In any free moment, God is waiting to be with you.

BLESSING

In the name of Jesus, I bless you with wonderful times of intimacy with the gracious, tender, passionate God. Whether short or long, may you rest in His presence and know the joy of being with Him.

—LINDA SHIN

AN INVITATION TO TELL SECRETS

SCRIPTURE

I wish I could go back to how things were a few months ago; when…God trusted me with his secrets! (Job 29:2,4 ISV)

COMMENT

A striking aspect of Jesus' ministry on earth was that He chose whom He would tell about the Kingdom of God. We tend to think of Jesus as sharing the gospel of the Kingdom with everybody, but that's not how He worked. In fact, when the disciples asked Him why He used parables with the people, He said, "*Because the knowledge of the secrets of the kingdom of heaven has been given to you, but not to them*" (Matt. 13:11). He spoke in parables to hide the Kingdom (see Luke 8:10).

So what qualifies you and me to hear the secrets of the Kingdom? Being Jesus' friend. Jesus told His disciples, "*I no longer call you servants, because a servant does not*

71

know his master's business. Instead, I have called you friends, for everything that I learned from my Father I have made known to you" (John 15:15).

In my quiet time a couple of weeks ago, I heard Him say that He wanted to take our friendship to the next level by having us share secrets with each other. He wanted me to tell Him my secrets, and He wanted to tell me His.

For Him and me, a big part of sharing secrets is telling each other our dreams—what seemingly impossible things each of us wants to happen. I sat with Him awhile, and as we talked about what I really wanted, He led me to think about some very wild goals. I asked Him what His dream was, and He said He dreams about unity among His people.

NEXT STEPS

1. Who was your best childhood friend? What secrets and dreams did you share with one another?

2. Get alone with God. Quiet your thoughts and spend some time just being with Him. Then tell Him that you want to share secrets with Him. Jesus, the best friend you'll ever have, wants to hear your secrets and to tell you His. He is giving you permission to tell Him the deepest longings of your heart, the things that you've wanted to happen for your whole life, the things that would bring

you the most joy. Then ask God what His dreams are.

3. You may find that, as this week progresses and you get more accustomed to sharing with Him, you think of more secrets to share with Him. And more secrets for Him to share with you. Give yourself and God time to tell these secrets.

BLESSING

I bless you, in Jesus' name, with even more intimacy as you and God share secrets. May you have the intimacy that this verse speaks of: "The Lord would speak to Moses face to face, as one speaks to a friend" (Exod. 33:11).

—RHOLAN WONG

FORGIVENESS

SCRIPTURE

Whenever you stand praying, if you have anything against anyone, forgive him [drop the issue, let it go], so that your Father who is in heaven will also forgive you your transgressions and wrongdoings [against Him and others]. [But if you do not forgive, neither will your Father in heaven forgive your transgressions] (Mark 11:25-26 AMP).

COMMENT

Forgiveness is a vital part of intimacy with God. If I am holding a grudge against someone else, it is very difficult to be completely open with God.

So what does forgiveness look like?

In my life, it has meant doing something very difficult. Like all of us, I have had woundings during my entire life.

It has meant spending a lot of time in SOZO inner healing sessions, digging deep to let go of wounds I have in my heart, soul, and mind.

And it has meant a long journey. But a journey worth every minute invested in it.

NEXT STEPS

1. Ask the Lord to show you who you need to forgive. People may come quickly to mind, or you may need to take your time in letting God reveal those who have hurt you. Write down the name of each person and ask God to show you how He sees that person and what He wants you to do.

2. Play a forgiveness game with the Lord. When someone hurts you, tell God that you are going to forgive them and pray blessings on them. God's part will be to work on that person on your behalf. As you do this, prepare to be surprised by the results.

3. Ask the Lord to heal your wounds from the unforgiveness in your life. Follow through when possible with a practical blessing for the people you have forgiven.

BLESSING

Lord Jesus, I pray that all those reading this will be made whole in Your call to forgiveness. I ask that they always look up to You and walk their wholeness out each day. I pray that they always look up to You and remember they are loved.

—SHEILA VERCIGLIO

SONG BRIDE

SCRIPTURE

The Lord your God is with you…He will take great delight in you; in His love He…will rejoice over you with singing (Zephaniah 3:17).

COMMENT

It is so amazing that our Bridegroom King has so many ways of speaking to us. One of the so-fun ways is through song. I think most of have been impacted by song, especially praise and worship songs. You see, our Bridegroom King wants an emotional tie—a spirit-to-spirit tie—to us. And music touches us in a special place there in our spirits.

He is a God who loves music. And because He created us in His image, our so-cool God designed us to enjoy music also. In fact, we can have a lot of fun with music in our relationship with Him. That's why, all through the Bible, we are encouraged to *"sing to him, sing praise to him; tell of all his wonderful acts"* (1 Chron. 16:9).

This past week, the Lord has been waking me up with a song. Sometimes it is the song that I went to sleep with or the song that I spent time hearing and singing the day before. Other times, it is a song that I haven't heard for a while. This morning, it was a song that He gave to me a while back:

> A new song I sing
>
> A song of praise and love and joy
>
> I sing to You, my beloved King of Kings.
>
> To the Lamb on the throne
>
> You will reign forever more
>
> I sing to You, my beloved King of Kings.
>
> To my Bridegroom so fair
>
> You are more than life to me
>
> I sing to You, my beloved King of Kings.

Whether the song is one you have just heard or a familiar one, we can sing these songs to our Bridegroom King and enter into a state of joyful intimacy with Him. Our day becomes a love song.

NEXT STEPS

1. When you wake up in the morning, pause and listen for a minute. Is there a song going through your mind?

2. If you can't hear all the words or you don't know the song, search the internet for "lyrics" and the words you can make out.

3. Download that song. Listen to it and sing with it throughout the day.

4. Take it as the song that your Bridegroom King has placed in your heart for the day. Enjoy it as your "together" song for the day, and sing it for your bridegroom lover.

BLESSING

I bless you to be a songbird and a song-bride for the King of Kings—to hear His song in your heart each morning and to carry His song for you throughout the day, singing and making melody in your heart to the Lord.

—Garland Cohen

GETTING DRUNK IN THE SPIRIT

SCRIPTURE

And don't get drunk with wine, which is rebellion; instead be filled with the fullness of the Holy Spirit (Ephesians 5:18 TPT).

All of them were filled with the Holy Spirit. … These people are not drunk (Acts 2:4,15).

COMMENT

As Christians, we can be supernaturally drunk. There is an infilling of the Holy Spirit that literally feels like intoxication. That's why the Acts 2 event appeared like drunkenness to onlookers.

In my experience, the key to being supernaturally drunk is cultivating a relationship with Holy Spirit. And as with human relationships, I get closer to Holy Spirit by spending time with Him, sharing intimate thoughts and feelings with Him and Him with me.

The first time I was spiritually drunk, I started with worship (see Ps. 100:4). I thanked Him for whatever came to mind. That brought me into His presence. Suddenly, I was filled with joy, because in His presence is unrestrained joy (see Ps. 16:11).

Even that first time, getting drunk wasn't difficult. It really was as easy as closing my eyes and visualizing Him standing right in front of me. Because He really is right here with me.

Then I just looked into His eyes and was willing to be undone by His gaze. This intimacy is the key to drinking Him in.

So, what is being supernaturally drunk like?

It's feeling emotionally undone, overtaken, wrecked.

It's being suddenly filled with waves of love, feeling loved right now just as I am.

It's an energy that infuses my body, soul, and spirit.

It's a careless surrender to falling deeper into communion with Holy Spirit.

But, mostly, it's joy. A joy that makes me feel like whatever is going on in my life at the time doesn't matter. In fact, I find I'm not really concerned at all with what is going on around me. It's a joy that overcomes inhibitions. In what might look like inappropriate enthusiasm, there can be spontaneous dancing, laughing, and singing. I like to call that "unreasonable joy."

Now, yes, many of those feelings are similar to the ones that come with drinking too much wine. But there's one key difference: spiritual drunkenness is feeling very close to God. So near that I sometimes see pictures of me worshiping Him in the throne room. It is as if I am caught up in the heavenly realm, in a different place, but here on earth at the same time.

I have found that, as I continue to drink more and more of Him, it has been easier and easier to be supernaturally intoxicated. So times alone with Holy Spirit have been less thinking and more drinking.

There's nothing like being in His presence, precious ones.

NEXT STEPS

1. Spend some time alone each day this week with Holy Spirit. Sit quietly with Him, and then think of five things that you are especially thankful for. Linger over this list, and then thank Him for each item.

2. Listen for anything He would tell you. He may bring to mind aspects of your five items that you hadn't thought of, like ways He has been working on your behalf. Or He may lead you to ask for even more in the area that He has already given to you in.

3. Allow yourself to feel close to God and receive what He has for you.

BLESSING

I bless you with encounters of love, communion, and intimacy with the King of Kings, Lord of

Lords, Elohim, Yahweh, Adonai, the Great I AM. I declare that you will get lost in His gaze and be filled with His Holy Spirit. I release and impart freedom to you to drink Him in and experience godly intoxication! May you be filled with unreasonable joy.

—Donna Sharou

MAKING GOD FAMOUS

SCRIPTURE

Lord! I'm bursting with joy over what you've done for me! My lips are full of perpetual praise. I'm boasting of you and all your works, so let all who are discouraged take heart. Join me everyone! Let's praise the Lord together. Let's make him famous! Let's make his name glorious to all. Listen to my testimony: I cried to God in my distress and he answered me. He freed me from all my fears! Gaze upon him, join your life with his, and joy will come. Your faces will glisten with glory. You'll never wear that shame-face again (Psalm 34:1-5 TPT).

COMMENT

Amen, let's "make Him famous."

We make Him famous by sharing the very best of what we have with each other. It is with great joy we open our hearts and freely give out our personal victories, healings, deliverances, joys, and anointings. I love to pray that everyone in the room get everything good that God has already given to me!

Thus I fulfill my desire to have people see and know Him. Wherever I go, as I bring God's good mood and great provision to those around me, those who have never had an encounter with the tender, gracious God learn firsthand that God loves them.

And we also make Him famous by cultivating and strengthening our connections with our church body. We are renewed, and other Christians around us are renewed, when we all give what we have been given and therefore enjoy and make known the wonders of our great King.

NEXT STEPS

1. As you read the preceding section, did Holy Spirit quietly bring to mind someone you can bless today? If so, ask Him to arrange a way for you to follow through on His prompting.

2. Intimacy with God also means talking and listening to Him throughout each day. I believe God prepares us and places before us each day opportunities to minister in some way to particular people. We may not be asked to speak to each one, but we have an anointing of some kind to impart through prayer, a prophetic word, or physical help. For example, we can stand by the joyful ones, laughing and imparting even more joy.

And we can stand with the despairing ones, crying with them and imparting comfort and peace. So ask Holy Spirit this week if there is someplace He has planned for you to be each day. Maybe He'll lead you to eat lunch at a different location. Or maybe He'll ask you to stop at a certain market on the way home. Ask, and you will receive His guidance.

BLESSING

I bless you right now with an intimacy and assurance that He is who He says He is and does what He says He will do. The results of your actions may not show up in this moment, and it may take even a few years for some prayers to fully be realized. But I bless you with a solid trust in His word for you.

Papa, please take all those reading this to the very center of Your heart for them. Keep them there and grant that they can live from this place of rest, joy, peace, and strength. Help them to stay intimate with You.

—Karen Reneau

LED INTO INTIMACY

SCRIPTURE

I hear the Lord saying, "I will stay close to you, instructing and guiding you along the pathway for your life. I will advise you along the way and lead you forth with my eyes as your guide. So don't make it difficult; don't be stubborn when I take you where you've not been before. Don't make me tug you and pull you along. Just come with me!" (Psalm 32:8-9 TPT)

COMMENT

I have a goal. I want to hear from God every day—in fact, multiple times a day.

I came to the School of Supernatural Ministry (SSM) with this goal in mind. Ever since I got saved, I have had a hunger to be with the Trinity and an earnest desire to know God deeply. Yet before SSM, my past was riddled with poor decisions based on misinterpreted prophetic impressions from others, as well as my misinterpreting prophetic words given to me.

I was in a lot of debt, struggled with numerous character faults, and generally lacked revelation or discipline in my relationship with God. Despite my good intentions, my poor decisions left me hurt enough that I didn't trust God and started to blame Him for much of what was going wrong in my life. I tried to hear from the Lord daily, but I heard Him speak to me maybe once a month. This life left me feeling like a failure.

I am happy to report that my life has changed dramatically. I learned I had built poor habits into my relationship with the Lord. First, I had to change my habit of obsessing over problems—whether my own or the problems of the world. Instead, I learned to let God speak to me about less weighty subjects. Then I could relax in His presence and risk not hearing clearly because the questions didn't seem as important or didn't require me to act upon His answers.

To rest and stop trying to solve all my problems along with those of the world was surprisingly difficult, but it felt like a breath of fresh air and soon set me on track to finding Him each day.

This was the first habit that the Lord changed in our relationship. In the next couple of entries, I want to take you deeper on the journey that I experienced so that you might meet the Lord daily, hear Him clearly, and be both powerful and free.

NEXT STEPS

In your devotional time, ask the Lord these questions:

1. Lord, do You love me?
2. Jesus, what do You like about me?
3. Father, why did You create me?

Ask these questions daily for one week. Write down the answers each day.

BLESSING

I bless you to know the Lord, to exchange ashes for a crown of beauty and a spirit of despair for a garment of praise.

—BRIAN BEESON

Led into Intimacy II

SCRIPTURE

Who, then, ascends into the presence of the Lord? And who has the privilege of entering into God's Holy Place? Those who are clean—whose works and ways are pure, whose hearts are true and sealed by the truth, those who never deceive, whose words are sure. They will receive the Lord's blessing and righteousness given by the Savior-God. They will stand before God. For they seek the pleasure of God's face, the God of Jacob (Psalm 24:3-6 TPT).

COMMENT

In my previous entry, I shared about a habit I needed to change. Instead of asking God about only very consequential issues, I learned to ask about things that seemed to have no significance. In other words, questions that didn't matter if they were answered one way or the other or even answered at all. I then found that I was slowly opening up to God and allowing my relationship with

Him to be more about Him and less about me. Because I was beginning to be set free from a religious spirit, this new approach felt revolutionary.

For years I had a fruitful prayer life, yet I never understood this deeper place of intimacy. I never bothered to enter into a give-and-receive relationship with the Lord, because I was caught up in prayer lists and exhaustive spiritual-warfare prayers.

Eventually, as I listened to Him without an agenda, He started confronting me on my behaviors. In a kind yet very firm way, He began to teach me how He valued me and thus soothed away my ambitions and insecurities. This process took months. Many days He would simply say that He loved me and nothing else. I struggled. Impatient, I would ask Him to tell me something else. In those moments, I eventually realized that I was falling into the same perspective of valuing only larger issues. I needed to completely and unrelentingly let go of this habit.

Once I was completely content in Him, He would begin to speak to me about the weightier things— Scripture, my behaviors and emotions, my friends, and my relationship with Him. If I tried to get information from Him, He would stop and let me wait until I had come back to a place of peace and submission. As we worked through this process, I soon learned to feel at ease. I could lay down the burden of trying to make something happen, to use my relationship with Him to achieve fruit or as a measure of my self-worth. I had even been caught up in using my relationship with God to advance my own ambitions in ministering to others.

When you begin to truly interact with Jesus, you'll learn quickly that He is clear yet gentle. And if you persist in being stubborn, He has more than enough patience to wait you out and more than enough kindness to encourage you to grow in love.

His love won my heart. Hearing Him declare His love over me day after day created a deep sense of security that allowed me to let go of so many things and exchange them for more of His love and words.

NEXT STEPS

1. Without abandoning your Bible reading or regular devotions, take plenty of time this week to listen to Him without deciding what the agenda should be. Truly let Him speak, and wait patiently until He does. (If He doesn't speak, simply repeat the questions from my previous entry. Allow the simplicity of His loving words to wash over you.)

2. Write down what He says, no matter how simple or insignificant you think it is.

BLESSING

I bless you to hear the voice of your Bridegroom and to enter into a divine romance that does not revolve around you. May your spirit awake to the joy of knowing your Beloved's thoughts and emotions.

—BRIAN BEESON

LED INTO INTIMACY III

SCRIPTURE

I had heard of you by the hearing of the ear, but now my eye sees you (Job 42:5 ESV).

COMMENT

In my previous entries, I briefly shared a journey of learning to release my need to set an agenda for my time with God. This letting go provided the critical mass for a rush of God into my life. Since that season, I have been more at ease with the Lord. Despite challenges and temptations that ever arise in my life, this understanding allows me to more fully trust Him and His timing. His silence no longer deters me. Instead of feeling discouraged by His unusual ways, I can wait to see what He will do and say.

This process started when I realized that I was mirroring the biblical cycle of the Old Testament priests in the tabernacle. Like those priests, I approached the Lord every day. On some days, He gave me what I could receive that day and nothing more. He might only say, "I love you," and then be silent. Yet I would then have enough for the day, like the priests who ate the daily showbread. Other days, He shared deep secrets with me. I directly encountered His presence, like the priest who entered the Holy of Holies.

As I learned to truly allow Him to say whatever He wanted, I discovered something else. When I took a risk to share a prophetic word or word of knowledge, I saw a dramatic increase in accuracy and effectiveness.

For example, one day I was worshiping at my church. At this point I had learned to just let myself bring my spirit to the Lord and *be* with Him. Just *be* with Him. Without needing to do anything. In fact, I didn't want to do anything besides just *be* with Him. In that place I heard the Lord ask me to share with a pastor friend of mine. We'll call him Jim. God wanted Jim to know that he was now using both sides of his brain. What an awkward word to give! However, because I received it while I was in such peace, I felt more confident in the word's authenticity and power. I shared the word with him.

Jim told me that a major international prophet had shared a dream with him years earlier. In the dream, the prophet had seen that half of Jim's brain was dead. He was only using one side of his brain. Jim received the word, and the Lord began to show him that there was much more that he needed to learn. Jim was faithful to grow, yet I'm sure he often wondered when the process would be complete and if the Lord would ever give him another word.

Well, God did! And it came through me! Jim told me that he was so thankful that I shared the word. Later I heard that he was sharing that story publicly because it had been such a powerful moment in his walk with the Lord.

By now I'm sure you see the point I was learning. When I allowed myself to be with the Lord and not insist that the relationship give me something, I could receive true and good words from God. Words that brought joy and freedom to my life and the lives of others because of their authenticity and truth.

NEXT STEPS

1. Spend time with the Lord without saying anything to Him. Just listen to Him and allow Him to fill your inward visions.

2. Write down what He speaks to you. Not to immediately share with someone else, but so you can take time to meditate on it and grow.

BLESSING

I bless you to be at peace. I take authority over distractions and wounds in your life that would cause you to deviate from pure and unwavering focus with Jesus, and I declare that you will know how to be His beloved and know your worth to Him.

—Brian Beeson

THE BEST MOTHER IN THE WORLD

SCRIPTURE

Because of your father's God, who helps you, because of the Almighty, who blesses you with blessings of the skies above, blessings of the deep springs below, blessings of the breast and womb (Genesis 49:25).

COMMENT

We are all pretty used to thinking of God as Father. And, indeed, Jesus encourages us to think of God this way. He continually refers to God as Father, perhaps most famously in His model prayer that begins, "Our Father." In fact, one of the reasons Jesus came to earth was to make God known to us as Father, the best Daddy we could have (see John 1:18).

But a friend recently explained to me that God can also be the best mother in the world. We get a clue to God's maternal side in "El Shaddai," one of the names

God gives Himself in the Old Testament. This name is usually translated "God Almighty." But others have pointed out that "El Shaddai" is more correctly translated "God [is] my breast."

I think God picked the name "El Shaddai" to show us an aspect of how He cares for us. I've heard mothers say that they feel the closest to their child when they are breastfeeding—when, skin to skin, they are giving him what he needs to survive.

Maybe God feels the closest to me when, in the most intimate connection, He is giving to me what I need. He delights to give me life—so much so that He suffers when He can't. I get a sense of what my refusal to receive feels like for the brokenhearted, maternal God when I read Jesus' anguished words over the Jews refusing Him. *"Jerusalem, Jerusalem, you who kill the prophets and stone those sent to you, how often I have longed to gather your children together, as a hen gathers her chicks under her wings, and you were not willing"* (Luke 13:34).

God delights in giving me what I need in my life, especially when I get close to Him and depend on Him. And my job often is not to try to give, but just to receive. Now certainly, as I mature, I will be able to give to Him and to others. But I will never outgrow my need to receive intimately from God.

NEXT STEPS

1. What are the ways that your earthly mother did a good job of nurturing you? What are

some ways that she fell a little short of what you needed from her?

2. All of us sometimes need someone else to express God's love to us. Particularly if you didn't receive the maternal nurturing you needed as a child, ask God to bring a spiritual mother to you.

3. In your time alone with God, ask Him to reveal Himself to you as your mother. Especially focus on the peaceful surrender that a nursing child has (see Ps. 131).

BLESSING

In Jesus' name, I bless you with a spirit of wisdom and revelation to know the maternal God's tender, loyal, and passionate love for you. Let it be. Amen.

—RHOLAN WONG

THE POWER OF PROPHECY

SCRIPTURE

The hand of the Lord was on me, and he brought me out by the Spirit of the Lord and set me in the middle of a valley; it was full of bones. He led me back and forth among them, and I saw a great many bones on the floor of the valley, bones that were very dry. He asked me, "Son of man, can these bones live?" I said, "Sovereign Lord, you alone know." Then he said to me, "Prophesy to these bones and say to them, 'Dry bones, hear the word of the Lord! This is what the Sovereign Lord says to these bones: I will make breath enter you, and you will come to life. I will attach tendons to you and make flesh come upon you and cover you with skin; I will put breath in you, and you will come to life. Then you will know that I am the Lord.'" So I prophesied as I was commanded. And as I was prophesying, there was a noise, a rattling sound, and the bones came together, bone to bone. I looked, and tendons and flesh appeared on them and skin covered them, but there was no breath in them. Then he said to me, "Prophesy to the breath; prophesy, son of man, and say to it, 'This is what the Sovereign Lord says: Come, breath, from the four winds and breathe into these slain, that they may live.'" So I prophesied as he commanded me, and breath entered them; they came to life and stood up on their feet—a vast army (Ezekiel 37:1-10).

COMMENT

Intimacy with God can sometimes mean hearing what God is declaring and then proclaiming those words also. This is what Ezekiel did.

Ezekiel faced a seemingly hopeless situation. To see a bone usually means something is very wrong. Much of the time we quickly associate a visible bone with extreme injury or even death. Even when eating, we know that a bone says it's time to get another piece of meat! "Dry" bones have no life, provide no nourishment, and have no value.

Yet the name Ezekiel means "God will strengthen." Ezekiel was to inspire and strengthen the generation that was born into exile and to remind them that the Lord God Almighty was still on their side.

So God tells Ezekiel to speak life to the dead bones that he sees before him. And when he does, the bones come to life, with flesh covering the bones and the breath of life in them. What's more, the dead bones without hope of life became a vast army of life—*for God!*

That's the kind of miracle that can happen when we are in an intimate relationship with God. Thanks to Holy Spirit living in us and the authority in Christ we possess, we too can hear what God is saying, declare it with Him, and see miracles.

Often, God invites us to speak His prophetic words. These words can be foretelling and forth-telling. Foretelling means I am telling you the future. Forthtelling means I am causing the future. (This is what God had Ezekiel do.)

Both of these kinds of prophecy will almost always show God's mercy and grace. What's the difference? Here's an example: You and I are going 100 miles per hour down the freeway. We get pulled over by a police officer who says, "You broke the law, and you're going to get a nasty ticket that might cost you your license." But then he says, "I'm going to forget it ever happened." That's mercy, or not getting what we deserve.

But the next thing he does is hand you $10,000 in cash. That's grace, receiving favor we don't deserve.

We have been given an abundance on top of being forgiven. That abundance is given so that we might have life "to the full" spiritually in God (John 10:10), and so that we might speak His mercy and grace to all those around us.

NEXT STEPS

1. What is God asking you to prophesy about right now? Ask Him and listen quietly for His answer.

2. Is there an area of your life that God wants to release new life into? What is "dead" that you know God wants to bring back to life? Now ask Jesus what He specifically wants you to declare in your situation just like He had Ezekiel declare in his valley of dry bones.

3. What are examples of God's mercy and God's grace in your life? I would encourage you to make a list of all of the instances that you can think of.

BLESSING

I bless you, in Jesus' name, with a deeper intimacy to hear His voice and a fresh revelation of the prophetic power of God in your life! May you partner with God and release life and breakthrough where it is needed. May you see what the world says is impossible become reality through your faithfulness in declaring the truth that God reveals to you in your circumstances. May you come to know firsthand the truth of what the angel Gabriel promises in Luke 1:37, "For nothing will be impossible with God" (NASB).

—ZAC KINTNER

DANCING WITH JESUS

SCRIPTURE

The one I love calls to me: Arise, my dearest. Hurry, my darling. Come away with me! I have come as you have asked to draw you to my heart and lead you out. For now is the time, my beautiful one. The season has changed, the bondage of your barren winter has ended and the season of hiding is over and gone. The rains have soaked the earth and left it bright with blossoming flowers. The season for singing and pruning the vines has arrived. I hear the cooing of doves in our land, filling the air with songs to awaken you and guide you forth (Song of Songs 2:10-12 TPT).

Trust in the Lord completely, and do not rely on your own opinions. With all your heart rely on him to guide you, and he will lead you in every decision you make. Become intimate with him in whatever you do, and he will lead you wherever you go. Don't think for a moment that you know it all (Proverbs 3:5-7 TPT).

COMMENT

I was staring at His extended hand. He was inviting me to join Him in a dance.

Wait…what was I hearing in the background? It sounded like a tango.

Why was He asking me to join Him in this particular dance? I don't know the tango!

And besides, isn't the tango, to say the least, an "inappropriate" dance for Jesus and me to be dancing? The tango's steps are extremely intricate and the movements are, uh, *intimate*. No, make that *veeerry intimate*. How could I even consider doing this dance with my Savior, my Lord?

All these thoughts swam through my head as I "politely" declined.

Yet, there He remained. I heard Him speak my name, making me look into His face. His eyes held my attention; they were like flames of fire. His arm, still extended with an open palm, spoke as well: "Won't you trust Me? Won't you let Me teach you this dance?"

Again, thoughts swirled in my head. My partner must be strong and steady to support me through the twists, turns, lifts, and other acrobatic movements in this dance. My goodness, He would have to lead. That meant I would be dancing backward and couldn't see where I was going. Would He be patient? I began to withdraw as I thought, "Oh my, can I trust You?"

He heard my unspoken words and began walking toward me. His gentle voice called to me: "Arise, My dearest! Hurry, My darling, come along with Me! I have come as you have asked. To draw you to My heart and lead you out! For now is the time, My beautiful one. The season has now changed. You are not in bondage, nor barren. You are free! You do not need to hide any longer. Come, learn of Me. There's so much I want to show you, so much I want you to know about Me, so much to share with you about My love for you."

Yes! I began to remember. I had asked my King, my Beloved, to teach me His ways, to show me His face. What I didn't expect was to learn the tango.

He was speaking again. "Beloved, won't you trust Me completely and not your own opinions? When you rely on Me with your whole heart, I will guide you. Become intimate with Me in everything you do, and I will lead you wherever you go."

I placed my hand in His. He twirled me under His arm and pulled me close—so close that a piece of paper between us could not have fallen to the ground.

I became uncomfortable as He began to lead me backward. I was scared; I couldn't see where we were going. I turned my head to see where He was leading. Uh oh, I'm losing my balance. I'm tripping! I was not in the right position. He gently repositioned me—my left hand on His shoulder, my face toward His, and my right hand in His. As I gazed into His eyes, my trust in Him increased, and I began to be comfortable with not seeing where I was going.

Each new step He taught me required a new level of trust and brought more healing and freedom. There were times I found myself irritably sensitive while learning these steps.

Unhealed areas were the cause of my agitation, and Jesus was relentless in His pursuit to make me whole.

His patient love, mercy, and grace, as I slowly learn to trust Him more, won me over. I continue to grow in my trust of Him as I learn more about my dance partner.

Most exciting is looking forward to intermediate and advanced dance classes. More and more intimacy is my desire. The adventure is here. Where will we go, whom will we meet, and what will we learn to do together?

NEXT STEPS

1. Watch some tangos and other dances. Note how the couple acts in unity while each one does his or her part.

2. As you think about dancing with Jesus, what do you think He wants you to experience? Love? Trust? Guidance? Joy? Something else?

3. Consider asking Jesus if there is a dance He would love to teach you so that you would become lifetime partners. If He asked you to dance, would you accept His invitation?

BLESSING

I bless you with an ever deeper intimacy with Jesus as you dance with Him. New levels of trust and joy be yours, in Jesus' name.

—Sheryl Beacon

DOCTRINE AND REVELATION

SCRIPTURE

You study the Scriptures diligently because you think that in them you have eternal life. These are the very Scriptures that testify about me, yet you refuse to come to me to have life (John 5:39-40).

COMMENT

In my devotional times, I'm sometimes tempted to rely on the written Word more than the spoken word. Reading the Bible quickly seems easier than calming my soul and waiting for God to speak to me. Reading means I have information right now; I don't have to wait. And reading means I get an unmistakable word; I don't have to guess whether that word is from God or just from me.

But just reading verses quickly without the Holy Spirit to make the words alive makes for a boring and restless morning. I benefit so much more when I read with an open heart to hear what God is saying to me in the Scripture that day. This kind of slow and active reading has led to some of my most intimate times with Him as He shows me what I could never have seen on my own. Many times, He has given me insights into my life that I never thought of or another way that He loves me.

I think of this experience this way: A love letter from my wife is certainly precious, and I would want to read it over and over. But my reading that letter will never match her reading that letter to me.

NEXT STEPS

1. In your devotional times this week, try asking God what scripture to read that day. Listen as He leads you to a particular chapter or verse.

2. Ask God to reveal Himself to you as you read the Bible. Be ready to receive in any way God chooses to express Himself. He may communicate with you through any of your five senses or by bringing thoughts to mind. Or He may give you a vision or a heavenly visitation.

3. Slowly read the scripture that God tells you about, maybe even reading it out loud a couple of times. Look for verses that stand out, ones that seemingly jump off the page.

BLESSING

In Jesus' name, I bless you with encounters with God through the Holy Scriptures this week. May your experiences of Him draw your heart ever closer to His heart. Let it be. Amen.

—RHOLAN WONG

GOD'S WORD

SCRIPTURE

Your word is a lamp to my feet and a light to my path (Psalm 119:105 NKJV).

Truth's shining light guides me in my choices and decisions; the revelation of your word makes my pathway clear (Psalm 119:105 TPT).

COMMENT

Oh, how I love the Word of God! When I'm struggling, hurting, or in need of comfort and direction, it is the place I go. It leads me into prayer and guides me into truth. Reading and studying the Bible gives me great pleasure, and yet in the busyness of life I sometimes neglect this Word that is so life sustaining.

There are times, too, when I listen to wonderful pastors and Bible teachers open the truth of God, and I neglect discovering truth from God Himself. Don't get me wrong—I need pastors and teachers to equip me, *and* I need to be taught by God with no middleman.

But when I sit down alone with God and His Word, there is more than teaching. There is communion and exchange. He gives me love so I can love him back. He gives me truth in exchange for the lies I'm believing. He gives me strength for my weakness, His joy for my sadness, His extravagant kindness to replace my fears, His presence to envelop me in His eternal goodness.

In Psalm 119, King David powerfully declares his love for the Word of God, bringing forth its truth, promises, and power. Listen to some of these truths and promises, and take them into your heart as your own.

God's Word:

> Is cleansing, bringing purity (verse 9)
>
> Is a guard against sin (verse 11)
>
> Revives the soul (verses 25, 107, 154)
>
> Strengthens the soul (verse 28)
>
> Gives the promise of mercies and salvation (verse 41)
>
> Gives answers when we are mocked (reproached) (verse 42)
>
> Is life giving and comforting (verse 50)
>
> Gives promises of grace and mercy (verse 58)
>
> Promises God will deal well with us (The Passion Translation refers to His *"extravagant kindness"*) (verse 65)
>
> Brings hope (verses 74, 81, 114, 147)

Is settled in heaven (The Passion Translation says *"standing firm in heavens and fastened to eternity"*) (verse 89)

Restrains us from evil (verse 101)

Guides us through life (verse 105)

Upholds us (strengthens our inner being) (verse 116)

Directs our steps (verse 133)

Is pure (verse 140)

Is always truth and endures forever (verse 160)

Causes us to be in awe of it (verse 161)

Causes us to rejoice (verse 162)

Gives understanding (verse 169)

Brings deliverance (verse 170)

In *The Chronicles of Narnia: The Lion, The Witch and the Wardrobe,* Lucy enters Narnia through a wardrobe closet and into one of the greatest adventures of her life. So it is when I sit down with the Word of God. I enter through the Word into a place that is as real as my physical reality to receive my identity, truths, and promises. The big difference between Narnia and the Word is that I can enter at will.

What extravagant goodness from God to give such an open invitation! Come anytime! Come often! And the more I enter in, the deeper the communion and the greater the adventure. I am in awe! Won't you join me?

NEXT STEPS

1. Enter into God's Word at least once each day this week. But try to enter as often as you can, whether you are reflecting on one verse, a chapter, or a book.

2. Each time you read the Bible, ask Father God to open your heart to the truths and promises in His Word.

3. Declare the list above to make the Bible's words your own.

BLESSING

Father God, I bless the readers abundantly, with open eyes of understanding to receive Your Word, allowing it to shape their characters to reflect You more and more. Meet them in the midst of Your Word, highlighting new revelations and promises. Amen.

—JUDI PETERSON

THE CALL OF THE LOVER

SCRIPTURE

As the branch cannot bear fruit by itself, unless it abides in the vine, neither can you, unless you abide in me (John 15:4 ESV).

COMMENT

This verse is always coming to me—usually several times a day. It has been coming to me for at least months and probably years. My natural inclination has been to interpret it as a need for self-effort. I must stay in the vine. I must bear fruit. *I must* try harder. But it took me until just recently to realize it for what it is. This verse is really Jesus, the Lover, calling me to Himself.

As the branch and the vine are one, as the husband and the wife are one flesh, He and I are one. There is no me without Him. There is no Him without me. We are one flesh.

And the great thing about being one with Him is that everything is done without self-effort because the great

Wooer and Lover is the Source of all things. For example, He is the source of my breath. And just as I breathe without thought or effort, so is His life-giving sap from the vine in me without my self-effort. Jesus doesn't make His lovers work.

I spoke with someone who had been healed of an eating disorder. She said her thinking had been that if she could just stop her habit for six months, then God would heal her. Then she realized that is just not the way God works. Once she stopped the self-effort, she realized some time later that her addiction had disappeared.

Once I took hold of this for myself, I determined that I would not, by force of will, try to overcome an addiction I had developed to a sudoku game on my phone. Not long after that, I had an encounter with Jesus, and I knew at the end of it that He had set me free from that addiction. Jesus doesn't make His lovers work.

NEXT STEPS

1. Listen for the love call of the Lord. Is there something that has been going through your head? Interpret that voice in your head as the wooing of the Lover.

2. Be aware of triggers that lead you to disconnect from God and to self-effort. Examples could be fatigue, urgent requests, or strict deadlines. Let your spirit gently refuse to be drawn into making something happen instead of focusing on oneness with Jesus.

3. Let Jesus be your Lover and your Healer. Take one thing in your life that you are attempting to change through self-effort. Ask the Lord to identify something if you don't already know it. Don't give in to self-effort on that item this week; just lay it at Jesus' feet and worship Him with it there before Him.

BLESSING

I declare the commanded blessings of the Lord will come upon you and overtake you (see Deut. 28:2), *and you will live in union with your Lover as his non-working bride.*

—GARLAND COHEN

WHEN GOD IS SILENT

SCRIPTURE

Now when John, while imprisoned, heard of the works of Christ, he sent word by his disciples and said to Him, "Are You the Expected One, or shall we look for someone else?" Jesus answered and said to them, "Go and report to John what you hear and see: the blind receive sight and the lame walk, the lepers are cleansed and the deaf hear, the dead are raised up, and the poor have the gospel preached to them. And blessed is he who does not take offense at Me" (Matthew 11:2-6 NASB).

COMMENT

So what do you do when God hasn't done what you expected Him to do?

That was certainly John's question. He had announced that Jesus was the Messiah, the one who would, according to Jesus' own words, "set the captives free." Yet there John was, languishing in prison. "So where's my freedom, Jesus? Because if You're not going to set me free, then

129

maybe You aren't the One I thought you were. Maybe I was wrong about You. Maybe I should look for someone else to deliver me."

Jesus responds to John's question in two ways. First, He tells him to look at the evidence. Jesus' work testified that He was the Messiah. And I'm in a much better spot if I look at what God is doing rather than focus on what He isn't doing.

He then asks John to not be offended that He hasn't freed him. And blessings come with that refusal to be offended. Instead of being offended because God hasn't helped me, I can continue to trust Him.

NEXT STEPS

1. Do you tend to think more about what God has done or what He hasn't done? The big question: Can you still be vulnerable and intimate with Him even if He hasn't met your expectations?

2. Think of a time in the past when God gave you either a different answer than you wanted or He didn't answer at all. Have you allowed a spirit of offense to turn you away from trusting Jesus?

3. In your secret place with Jesus, be completely honest with Him about the things He hasn't yet done for you. (You might find reading some of the Psalms, such as Psalm 13, helpful as you join with David in his

laments.) Without that kind of honesty, intimacy is very difficult. Wait for Him to respond to you.

BLESSING

I bless you with an open heart to tell God what you're feeling and open ears to hear what He wants to tell you. In the name of Jesus, let it be. Amen.

—RHOLAN WONG

KNOW WHAT
YOU CARRY

SCRIPTURE

So God created man in his own image, in the image of God he created him; male and female he created them (Genesis 1:27 ESV).

COMMENT

Has anyone ever told you they felt a certain way whenever you come around? Or have you ever asked Holy Spirit what you carry as a person? Did you know that you are meant to release what you carry into the atmosphere?

Before I knew to even ask any of these questions, I started noticing how my friends or people I prayed for would tell me they felt such peace or would feel like they're in a garden when I was praying for them. I just brushed off their comments as them experiencing God's Presence.

But one day a speaker invited me to ask Holy Spirit what I carry and to know that is what I release into the atmosphere just by being who I am! God created each of us with different attributes of Him, such as His love, joy, and peace. We are to know what we carry so that we can partner with Him by releasing what is needed in an environment.

When I asked God what I carry, I heard peace and the Garden of Eden experience. Funny how I was already pouring that out without even knowing! How much more powerful can I be now that I know what I release!

This experience is for you as well. When God's children walk in what they carry, we release this into the atmosphere, and this world is forever changed!

NEXT STEPS

1. Spend some time with Holy Spirit this week and ask Him what you carry. Write down what He says.

2. At least three times this week, practice proactively releasing what you carry. Your action can be as simple as saying, "In Jesus' name, I release _____ to you" (or "in this place"). Release it when you are one on one with someone and/or in a corporate setting such as worship.

3. Don't be surprised when people see a difference according to what you carry. Thank God and rejoice that He has chosen you to demonstrate an aspect of His character.

BLESSING

Father God, thank You for creating us in Your image. Thank You that You have created us all to hold different attributes of You and that we can partner with You to release them to others as well as into the atmosphere. I pray that You will reveal to the person reading this what they carry and how You want to partner with them in order to release it. I bless them with the revelation of how powerful You've made them. In Jesus' name, amen.

—MINDY RIVAS

INTIMATE WORSHIP

SCRIPTURE

In the neighborhood there was an immoral woman of the streets, known to all to be a prostitute. When she heard about Jesus being in Simon's house, she took an exquisite flask made from alabaster, filled it with the most expensive perfume, went right into the home of the Jewish religious leader, and knelt at the feet of Jesus in front of all the guests. Broken and weeping, she covered his feet with the tears that fell from her face. She kept crying and drying his feet with her long hair. Over and over she kissed Jesus' feet. Then she opened her flask and anointed his feet with her costly perfume as an act of worship (Luke 7:37-38 TPT).

COMMENT

What does intimate worship look like? One example is the woman in Luke 7.

Intimate worship looks like shamelessness. The woman didn't care that Jewish society would have never accepted a woman inviting herself to a Pharisee's home, much less when he was hosting guests, and much, much less when that woman was a prostitute.

And intimate worship can also look like wasteful sacrifice. She lavishes the most costly perfume on Jesus. She doesn't reserve any of it or use a cheaper scent.

Intimate worship often looks at least different and maybe offensive from what I'm used to. She changes three major customs of the day. She washes Jesus' feet, not with water, but with her tears; she kisses, not His cheek, but His feet; and she anoints His head, not with oil, but with perfume. Perfume in those days was often used by prostitutes (see Prov. 7:17), yet Jesus accepts this offering from her anyway. Unconcerned about the social mores she is turning on their heads, she is thinking only about how she can express her adoration.

Finally, intimate worship doesn't have to use words. She silently adores Jesus.

NEXT STEPS

1. Read the story of the woman's worship several times slowly, including a couple of times out loud. Let yourself feel what the woman must have felt as she was there before Jesus.

2. Think about whether you sometimes hold back from worshiping God because you feel unworthy, or you're wondering what people might think, or you don't know what to do. Resolve to worship no matter what happens,

secure in the knowledge that God wants and accepts your heartfelt praise.

3. The next time you are worshiping God in a church service, focus solely on Jesus. You may find yourself not even aware of the people around you.

4. The next time you are worshiping God alone, express your worship in a way that you haven't done before. You might dance, or shout for joy, jump up and down, or do something you've never seen anyone else do.

5. At another time that you are worshiping privately, sit or lie down and say nothing. Express your adoration without words; instead, act out your devotion.

BLESSING

In the name of Jesus, I bless you with a new level of freedom and intimacy as you worship Jesus. Let it be. Amen and amen.

—RHOLAN WONG

CRY OF THE BRIDE

SCRIPTURE

Come walk with me…. Come taste the fruits of Your life in me (Song of Songs 4:16 TPT).

COMMENT

God relates to us in many ways: Master, Teacher, Friend, and Father. But, most precious to me, God is my Bridegroom King.

This verse became the cry of my heart for weeks and weeks. It is still the cry of my heart to be one with my beloved Jesus. It is the cry of a bride whose passion for her Bridegroom King is only growing stronger and stronger each passing day. It is the heart cry that Jesus heard and responded to.

The day came when, after starting and stopping several times, I finally made up my mind to accept the invitation of the Bridegroom King.

Until the darkness disappears and the dawn has fully come. In spite of shadows and fears, I will go to the mountaintop with you—the mountain of suffering love and the hill of burning incense. Yes, I will be your bride (Song of Songs 4:6 TPT).

Life has not been the same since, taking twists and turns I could have never planned on my own. Some exciting, some frightening, always stretching my faith, always with the call of the Bridegroom King continually saying, "You are beautiful, my equal, my bride. You have ravished my heart! Come away with me!"

I'm no longer looking back, but put my hand in the hand of my Lover, singing with Him:

Arise, my darling! Come quickly my beloved. Come and be the graceful gazelle with me. Come be like a dancing deer with me. We will dance in the high place of the sky, yes, on the mountains of fragrant spice! Forever we shall be united as one! (Song of Songs 8:14 TPT)

Won't you do the same? I invite you to begin your own journey of the bride.

NEXT STEPS

1. Begin your own journey of the bride by reading Song of Songs in *The Passion Translation.*

2. Read devotionally. For example, after reading a passage, stop and worship, singing the Scriptures to the Lord.

3. For more depth of understanding, read *The Sacred Journey: God's Relentless Pursuit of Our Affection* by Brian Simmons.

BLESSING

May you discover the unrelenting, passionate love of Jesus as you take the sacred journey of the immature young maiden who is transformed into the mature, passionate Bride. God bless you richly and abundantly as you open your heart to your true love!

—JUDI PETERSON

EMBRACING THE MYSTERY OF OUR GOD

SCRIPTURE

As soon as all the people saw Jesus, they were overwhelmed with wonder and ran to greet him.

"What are you [the disciples] arguing with them [teachers of the law] about?" he asked.

A man in the crowd answered, "Teacher, I brought you my son, who is possessed by a spirit that has robbed him of speech. Whenever it seizes him, it throws him to the ground. He foams at the mouth, gnashes his teeth and becomes rigid. I asked your disciples to drive out the spirit, but they could not."

"You unbelieving generation," Jesus replied, "how long shall I stay with you? How long shall I put up with you? Bring the boy to me."

So they brought him. When the spirit saw Jesus, it immediately threw the boy into a convulsion. He fell to the ground and rolled around, foaming at the mouth.

Jesus asked the boy's father, "How long has he been like this?"

"From childhood," he answered. "It has often thrown him into fire or water to kill him. But if you can do anything, take pity on us and help us."

"'If you can'?" said Jesus. "Everything is possible for one who believes."

Immediately the boy's father exclaimed, "I do believe; help me overcome my unbelief!"

When Jesus saw that a crowd was running to the scene, he rebuked the impure spirit. "You deaf and mute spirit," he said, "I command you, come out of him and never enter him again."

The spirit shrieked, convulsed him violently and came out. The boy looked so much like a corpse that many said, "He's dead." But Jesus took him by the hand and lifted him to his feet, and he stood up.

After Jesus had gone indoors, his disciples asked him privately, "Why couldn't we drive it out?"

He replied, "This kind can come out only by prayer [several translations add 'and fasting']" (Mark 9:15-29).

COMMENT

I heard Bill Johnson speak on this scripture at a conference, and his message really stayed with me. Not because the disciples failed to cast out the demon, but rather because this story shows me what to do when my prayers are ineffective.

The disciples had evidently been used to seeing demons expelled when they and Jesus prayed. Perhaps up to that time, they had had a 100 percent success rate.

The disciples knew that Jesus is the King of the Kingdom of Heaven. They had seen that, when His Kingdom collides with earthly realms, His Kingdom wins. When His Kingdom confronts sickness or torment, those things must go.

So I can understand their confusion when their prayers didn't work. But there is a very important element of the story that most believers often miss. The point is this: When there is no answer to prayer, I need to take Jesus aside and talk with Him about it.

Like the disciples, I can ask Jesus, "What happened? Why didn't this work?"

Still, in my desire for a comfortable answer, I have to be careful not to make the disciples' answer a spiritual formula. For the disciples, the answer here was prayer and fasting. However, that might not be the answer for me.

But I can know that the answer is always found in Jesus. The heart of all that I do for the Kingdom of God is rooted in an intimate relationship with God Himself. More than anything else, our Lord wants to deepen my intimacy with Him. I need to be able to, like the disciples, approach Jesus when the child isn't healed and ask Him how I can understand what He's doing and what the solution is.

What I cannot do is adjust my thinking to accept unanswered prayers as the new normal. I think that one of the biggest problems in the North American church is that we are uncomfortable with the reality of the mystery of God. The truth is that in this life there is mystery that I cannot understand or explain about the things of God. The best thing for me to do in those times is to go to Jesus directly for answers and clarity, not change my theology to match a bad experience. My theology should always reflect the truth of Scripture, even in the midst of disappointment. I believe that as I press in, my experience will match my theology if I'm willing to fight for what I know to be true!

In this story, the disciples exemplify a lifestyle that we believers can embrace. We are on a journey of growing in understanding of what it means to live a Christian life. The things of God are now becoming the things that are the desire of our lives. Jesus brought the Kingdom of God to earth and now that is also our mission—to help people understand and experience the Lordship of Jesus.

But it's a journey, not an overnight success story. And God invites us into the mystery of unanswered prayer in our journey. As believers, we're slowly learning how to live out what is revealed in Scripture.

NEXT STEPS

1. Think of a time when you prayed for something that didn't happen. Ask Jesus about that instance and why your prayer didn't affect the situation. How does what He says change the way that you now interpret that experience?

2. Did you become frustrated with God or doubt your faith when you didn't see manifest what you were praying for? Have you spoken to Him about that? I would encourage you to speak with Him now and to forgive yourself or anyone else who might have been hurt as a result of how you interpreted that challenging experience. You might even have to forgive Him for not answering you when you wanted Him to.

BLESSING

I bless you, in Jesus' name, with a heart to go to Jesus with the supernatural mysteries of life as we pursue the Kingdom of Heaven here on earth. I pray Ephesians 1:17 over you, "I keep asking that the God of our Lord Jesus Christ, the glorious Father, may give you the Spirit of wisdom and revelation, so that you may know him better."

—Zac Kintner

Romance with Jesus

SCRIPTURE

My people are destroyed for lack of knowledge. Because you have rejected knowledge, I also will reject you from being priest for Me (Hosea 4:6 NKJV).

COMMENT

The word "knowledge" used here is a derivative of the same word that explains how Adam "knew" Eve, and she conceived. This "knowledge" is the very deepest intimacy. I feel God is saying here "without intimacy with Me, my people will perish." We have to become the bride. When I share that with other men, I see them flinch a little. I can almost read their minds. "But God's a dude and that is weird, man. I don't get it."

Okay. I understand. At first it was awkward for me as well. But men (and women too), hang in there with me for a moment and I will explain. During various prayer times, I would ask the Holy Spirit to teach me how to be intimate with God. How to get closer and see His face.

I would hear the Holy Spirit say, "Become His lover." "Whoa! That's weird. I rebuke that." It was really uncomfortable, and to be honest, it creeped me out a little bit.

The next prayer time I had, the Holy Spirit said, "Are you ready to become His lover?" I hesitated and ignored the Holy Spirit, pretending what I was doing was good enough. Yet I would get around other students in the School of Supernatural Ministry, and we would talk about how we wanted more of God. Then I would get to my prayer time and resist the Holy Spirit showing me how to get more of God.

After about a week of fighting and trying to ignore the Holy Spirit, I gave up and said, "Okay, Holy Spirit, show me how." I heard the Holy Spirit say, "Romance Him." What! *Nope*, not doing that! I tried casting the Holy Spirit out of my prayer time. Obviously, that didn't work. After a couple of days of fighting the Holy Spirit again and losing, I surrendered. I said, "Okay, Holy Spirit, I trust You and love You, but please don't make me look foolish or humiliate me." For some reason, I knew this romantic place was where my heart would really be open. I was going to become vulnerable, hence the request of "don't humiliate me." The Holy Spirit didn't, but He did show me how to romance God.

The Holy Spirit showed me that intimacy starts when two lovers stare into each other's eyes and share what they love about each other. But now coming from a male perspective, the man will usually start off with how pretty he thinks his lover is by complimenting, for example, her hair, eyes, or shape. But a deeper intimacy comes when he compliments her character or thanks her for loving, encouraging, and believing in him. That next day she may wake up with no makeup, messy hair, and morning breath. But he can still leave the house with thoughts in his heart of how he loves her character and appreciates her love for him.

In the same way, men, do you see you don't have to get caught up in the physical aspect of your God romance? You can still open up your heart to God. The Holy Spirit reminded me of when my father was on his deathbed, and I would sit next to him and talk. He was quite frail, but I never mentioned his physical condition. Instead, I told him I appreciated how he took care of me and what that care meant to me. I told him his example showed me how big his heart was toward me and others and how that realization changed my outlook on life.

I realized I can say to God the same thing I said to my father many years ago: "Thank you for taking care of me, and I love how you look out for me. I also love how you love me when I don't love myself."

Men and women, do whatever it takes to get over any hindrances or hang-ups for this relationship. It will be worth it.

NEXT STEPS

1. How have you attracted the opposite sex? What has worked the best for you? If

appropriate, how would you apply that approach to Jesus?

2. In current or past relationships, what have you done to keep the romance alive? Again, can you apply any of those actions to your relationship to Jesus?

3. Romance takes time. In your devotional time with Jesus this week, give the two of you enough time to be close.

BLESSING

In Jesus' name, I bless you with wisdom to know how to romance your Lover. And I bless you with a playfulness as you try out different approaches to the One who loves you. More intimacy, Holy Spirit, this week for the Lover and His beloved. Amen.

—STEVE PERKINS

SEDUCTION

SCRIPTURE

It is because of him [God] *that you are in Christ Jesus, who has become for us wisdom from God— that is, our righteousness, holiness and redemption* (1 Corinthians 1:30).

COMMENT

Seduce—to tempt to wrongdoing. Synonyms—decoy, tempt, bait, lure, and lead astray. Antonyms—protect, preserve, guide. (Webster's Dictionary)

Seduction is a powerful influence on the body of Christ. It's an alluring alternative to waiting and trusting for that answer to prayer or to a divine promise that confirms our faith in Someone real.

We are all waiting on God for something. As our culture champions the big dreamers and rewards the brave, we dig deeper into the possibilities of our future. But with that boldness to dream comes the devil's predictable tactic of seduction, which entices us to compromise the best for what's available now.

I recently found myself in a very awkward, uncomfortable situation that would have been very difficult to escape. While I wasn't led astray, I had to answer these questions assaulting my mind as I resisted each advance. Why not? What's the harm? Is that really what God wants for me? Does God really care if I mess up a little? Why can't I have just a little fun?

I knew that the option wasn't the best for me. But it was at least *something*. And it was something I wanted. It just wasn't in the right package from God.

While I didn't feel tempted to take the bait, it did make me feel sad because I was still waiting on the promise. It was in this state of forlorn victory that God showed me I was experiencing seduction. I had subtle doubts that begged me to reconsider the high ideals I set for myself. I was looking at the beginning of compromise.

The Lord took me to Proverbs 7, where the seductress tells her victim of all she has prepared for him to meet his needs and desires. It's alluring, but it's a decoy, a trap, and a false promise.

Satan always uses an ounce of truth to get us to swallow a lie. Whether Eve in Eden, Jesus in the desert, or me right now, satan seductively offers what God has already promised to us. He uses our longings, desires, calling, or birthright to tempt us to take it now instead of waiting for the real thing. But Father God, already knowing the weapons the enemy would use, gave us protection from this trap.

Specifically, He gave us wisdom.

Do not forsake wisdom, and she will protect you; love her, and she will watch over you. The beginning of wisdom is this: Get wisdom. Though it cost all you have, get understanding. Cherish her, and she will exalt you; embrace her, and she will honor you. She will give you a garland to grace your head and present you with a glorious crown (Proverbs 4:6-9).

Webster's dictionary lists wisdom as an antonym to seduction. In the process of receiving your promise, you will be given opportunities to lower your standards. In your intimate place with God, call on His wisdom to equip you as you trust in His truth and purposes for your life.

NEXT STEPS

1. Ask Jesus to reveal Himself to you as wisdom. What is He showing you? Is this different from what you expected? How?

2. Seduction doesn't have to be sexual, although many times it is. It can look like anything that satisfies your appetite. But if you give in, you'll discover that it doesn't fill or satisfy your soul. Ask Jesus to show you if or how the enemy is using seduction to harm you.

3. Ask Jesus how to partner with wisdom when it comes to the deepest desires of your heart. It's in the place of vulnerability that we need His protection and wisdom. Don't let go of what He shows you or tells you. The wisdom He gives you will be your guide.

BLESSING

I bless your dreams, the ones you're still waiting to see come true and the ones buried so deep only Jesus knows about them. They all matter. And they all need the wisdom of Jesus to get us through the process and into the promise. I bless you with wisdom to resist seduction and false promises. I bless you to be wisdom for others who are struggling. I bless your process, and I bless you.

—TENESSA AUDETTE

SEEING AND LOVING WITH GOD'S HEART

SCRIPTURE

God always blesses those who are kind to the poor and helpless. They're the first ones God helps when they find themselves in any trouble. The Lord will preserve and protect them. They'll be honored and esteemed while their enemies are defeated. When they are sick, God will restore them, lying upon their bed of suffering. He will raise them up again and restore them back to health (Psalm 41:1-3 TPT).

COMMENT

Intimacy with God will inevitably lead to caring for the needy around us. When we experience God gently but passionately loving us, the result is that we love others. As John tells us, *"We love because He first loved us"* (1 John 4:19).

What does this love look like?

It is selfless. God loved us even when we were rebelling against Him, and we love others who do not love us back and can do nothing for us.

It initiates. "God first loved us." He didn't wait for us to make the first move; He loved us before we ever moved toward Him.

It gives. "*This is how God showed his love among us: He sent his one and only Son into the world that we might live through him*" (1 John 4:9). God loved; therefore, He gave.

When we love this way, we align ourselves with God's heart for the world. And as a bonus, we experience a new level of intimacy with Him as we see what He is doing and hear what He is saying and then partner with Him in loving the world.

NEXT STEPS

1. This may sound like a silly question, but have you experienced God's love? Have you heard Him tell you what He thinks of you? If you're not sure, ask God this week to tell you something new about how He loves you. Tell Him you're not satisfied with just knowing intellectually that He loves you. You want an experience of His love.

2. Let God's love so fill your heart that you can begin asking Him to teach you how to love others. You might start by asking Him to show you how He sees, and loves, the people around you.

3. Remember that when you walk into a room, you are walking in with Him. You carry His living presence, kindness, and love inside of you to share.

BLESSING

I bless you this week with new eyes and ears to see and hear how God loves you. And I bless you with a heart to honor every opportunity to be who you are to the poor around you. Whether they are lacking in wealth and status or in love and peace, or even if they are caught in the most treacherous sin, I bless you with loving how God has loved you. Holy Spirit, fill all those reading this so they can see what You see, hear what You are saying, and love as You are loving the world. Let them know Your love so well that they cannot resist being Your loving and helping hand.

—KAREN RENEAU

IMITATING GOD

SCRIPTURE

See what great love the Father has lavished on us, that we should be called children of God! And that is what we are! (1 John 3:1)

COMMENT

So, what really leads to living a holy life?

Well, Jesus had a simple plan for His life: He just said what He heard the Father saying and did what He saw His Father doing. (See John 12:50 and John 5:19-20.)

Now due to my legalistic church upbringing, I can easily interpret these statements as commands. I must monitor my actions very carefully and ensure that I say and do only the right things.

But I'm pretty sure that Jesus thought of His life a little differently. He didn't have a list of things He could and couldn't do. Knowing His Father's love and out of the relationship They had, the Son—like all sons—just wanted to be like His Daddy.

During my intimate times with Him, as I know the Father's love in a deeper and deeper way, I will more and more be like Him. And if those times reveal what He is saying and doing, I will know what to work on Him with. Let it be.

NEXT STEPS

1. Legalism has infected just about everyone. If you want to be more free, Galatians 3 through 5 may help. Hold on to Galatians 5:1: *"It is for freedom that Christ has set us free. Stand firm, then, and do not let yourselves be burdened again by a yoke of slavery."*

2. Ask God to show you something new about His love for you. And then just let yourself soak in His love.

3. Then ask Him to show you what He is saying and doing today. Out of all the good things He is saying and doing, what specifically is He up to right now in your life? And what is He telling you about how to cooperate with Him?

BLESSING

In Jesus' name, I bless you today with an intimacy to know His tenderness toward you and how He is acting with you in this world right now.

—Rholan Wong

Week 39

AUTHORITY IN JESUS BY OUR DECLARATIONS

--- SCRIPTURE ---

Listen to the truth I speak to you: If someone says to this mountain with great faith and having no doubt, "Mountain, be lifted up and thrown into the midst of the sea," and believes that what he says will happen, it will be done (Mark 11:23 TPT).

Truly I tell you, if anyone says to this mountain, "Go, throw yourself into the sea," and does not doubt in their heart but believes that what they say will happen, it will be done for them (Mark 11:23).

The mountain and the sea can also be metaphors. Mountains in the Bible can refer to kingdoms, and the sea can represent the nations, i.e., "sea of humanity." Faith lifts up and brings more than hyperbole; it is the active power of faith to take with us and carry the power and authority of the mountain-kingdom of God wherever we go.

COMMENT

I want to encourage you to know your authority in our Lord Jesus as His children. You may be thinking this is "way too deep" or "I'm not there yet!" I believe all followers of Jesus have said this more than once in their walk with Him.

The Lord has been speaking to me about my authority as His child for the past six months and confirmed it as I was reading the above verse in my TPT and NIV Bibles. It's not that I deserve this authority, but I receive it because of His goodness. He made me one with Him when He sealed me by His Holy Spirit, so I carry His authority. And He longs for me to walk in my divine authority!

Here are some verses that tell us more about this authority.

And these signs will accompany those who believe: In my name they will drive out demons; they will speak in new tongues; they will pick up snakes with their hands; and when they drink deadly poison, it will not hurt them at all; they will place their hands on sick people, and they will get well (Mark 16:17-18).

Very truly I tell you, whoever believes in me will do the works I have been doing, and they will do even greater things than these, because I am going to the Father. And I will do whatever you ask in my name, so that the Father may be glorified in the Son (John 14:12-13).

His incomparably great power for us who believe. That power is the same as the mighty strength he exerted when he raised Christ from the dead and seated him at his right hand in the heavenly realms (Ephesians 1:19-20).

Now to him who is able to do immeasurably more than all we ask or imagine, according to his power that is at work within us (Ephesians 3:20).

As we spend time with Him and grow in our intimacy, He reveals truth in our spirit-man. It gets to the point that it's no longer us trying to know Him better. It's Him who's giving us the Spirit of revelation and His deepest secrets. All He is waiting for is you!

NEXT STEPS

1. Meditate on the above scriptures until you feel your mind and your spirit saying yes to your position of authority. You may want to read the verses out loud and slowly several times for a few days.

2. I suggest starting with baby steps in your declarations. For example, choose declarations of daily activities. When I began practicing my authority, I declared that

I would have a parking space close to the entrance of the mall.

3. Keep making declarations, no matter what the results are. I have declared things that I haven't seen immediately—for example, a favored life for my children. But I don't let that discourage me. I just keep exercising my authority and making declarations. I need to settle in my heart that I will unconditionally trust God because He knows what's best for me. To this day, I find that things happen more for me as I declare them.

4. Give thanks in every declaration and when you see the results. Declare your faith in God that He is working according to His will!

BLESSING

I bless you as you continue to pursue your authority in Him! May you find His beauty, His goodness, and most of all His deep love for you as you increase in your intimacy with our great and awesome God!

—RUTH KUIZON

THE PAST IS MEANT TO BE JUST THAT—THE PAST!

SCRIPTURE

But I, yes I, am the one who takes care of your sins—that's what I do. I don't keep a list of your sins (Isaiah 43:25 MSG).

COMMENT

Do you ever find yourself looking back regretting mistakes you made? Or wish you could go back and tell your younger self that you are way more valuable than you allowed yourself to believe back then?

If you do, you are not the only one! However, these moments are exactly what satan uses against us to prevent us from moving forward in our destinies. He wants us to believe that we've made too many mistakes, that we're not "good" enough to do the amazing things that God has created us for.

I have struggled and continue to struggle with negative thoughts about myself, but I am learning how to take control of my thoughts and no longer allow the negative thoughts to dictate my life. I was created for so much more, and so were you!

If God chooses not to remember our sins, then who are we to keep beating ourselves up because of them? Jesus came to pay the price for our sins, and we can honor and glorify His sacrifice by letting our past be our past and moving forward into what He is calling us to!

NEXT STEPS

1. Choose to forgive your younger self for the mistakes made in the past. This can be a powerful tool for letting go and moving forward. If you haven't, ask Jesus to also forgive you and to help you move on from your sins.

2. If you struggle with negative thoughts, begin to read Scripture out loud, declaring who you are in Christ, especially when those thoughts begin to torment you. For example, meditate on Matthew 11:11: *"Truly I tell you, among those born of women there has not risen anyone greater than John the Baptist; yet whoever is least in the kingdom of heaven is greater than he."* And First Peter 2:9-10: *"But you are a chosen people, a royal priesthood, a holy nation, God's special possession, that you may declare the praises of him who called you out of darkness into his wonderful light.*

Once you were not a people, but now you are the people of God; once you had not received mercy, but now you have received mercy."

3. Whenever you are feeling negative about yourself, spend time in worship. Ask Jesus to come and show you who you are to Him and, if you have a hard time believing it, ask Him to help you let it sink in deep into your heart, mind, soul, and spirit.

BLESSING

Beautiful Jesus, I ask that You would flood each and every person reading this with Your love. Speak to them words of affection and help them to go deep in their hearts. Thank You for loving us more than we could ever love ourselves, and thank You that Your perfect love casts out all fear. I bless each and every one of them with encounters from Heaven that will speak to them about who they are and who they are meant to be in the Kingdom of God. Release the spirit of adoption over them now in Your mighty Name. Amen.

—MINDY RIVAS

AFTERWORD

Congratulations on finishing this forty-week journey of intimacy with God.

So, what's next?

Even more intimacy with God.

Because two things are true: No matter how much intimacy we have with God, there still remains a deeper, closer intimacy with an infinite God. And our loving God is always pursuing more intimacy with us.

So maybe God will lead the Southern California School of Supernatural Ministry to write a second book on intimacy. Or maybe someone reading these words will write that book!

I bless you with more and more glory as you spend intimate time with your God face to face.

And we all, who with unveiled faces contemplate the Lord's glory, are being transformed into his image with ever-increasing glory, which comes from the Lord, who is the Spirit (2 Corinthians 3:18).

—RHOLAN WONG

APPENDIX

Just in case you need more devotionals to take you beyond 40 weeks, here are four more readings.

WHEN GOD ASKS YOU TO DO THE HARD THINGS

For though the mountains should depart and the hills be shaken or removed, yet My love and kindness shall not depart from you, nor shall My covenant of peace and completeness be removed, says the Lord, Who has compassion on you (Isaiah 54:10 AMPC).

COMMENT

When I began the journey of doing one of the hardest things God has ever asked me to do, my marriage was completely broken. I was basically a single mom caring for a newborn for the first time. I thought I was on the path to divorce and would be raising my daughter alone.

One night as I was up with my daughter for her nightly feeding, I was crying out to God about what was going on and, as clear as if it had actually been His audible voice, I heard, "What if I could save your marriage and make it better than you could ever have imagined it to be?"

I was shocked. First, I knew that wasn't a thought that would come from myself at that time. Second, given the circumstances I faced, I couldn't believe that God was actually asking me to fight for my marriage rather than walk away from it. Yet, from that night forward, I knew in my heart that I needed to stand and fight for my marriage.

This was not an easy fight. I often told God that I couldn't do it anymore. The pain was just too great. I didn't really have any hope that what He spoke to me would come to pass.

In those moments, God would show me a picture, send me a dream, or send me an encouraging person to reaffirm that He was fighting for my family just like He promised. And so I would once again find the strength to keep up the good fight. Then, all of a sudden, a little over two years after my marriage came crashing down, my husband came home just like God had promised me he would!

Now, don't misunderstand. Life has not been easy. We are still on the journey of reconciliation and restoration. But, as I write this, God has been faithful once again to His promise to me, and I am expecting our second child this fall!

He is a good and faithful Father who longs to work with us to fulfill His promises. He just asks that we will trust Him to see those promises through to completeness. And, yes—He will do this for you, too!

NEXT STEPS

1. Has God asked you to do something hard? Find a group that will hold you up in prayer and will walk with you during the process. My group of friends was a Godsend during my hard time.

2. Ask God to bring someone to you who has gone through a similar hard time. Be vulnerable with him or her. I am beyond thankful for my friends who helped me to be strong when I felt the weakest. They let me be real and honest with them about how I felt. They also made me feel safe, because I knew they loved me enough that they wouldn't gossip about what I was going through.

BLESSING

I bless you with the strength to do the hard things when God asks you to. I bless you with dreams and visions to help you through the process of walking through the hard thing. I bless you with peace and joy even when your circumstances seem the darkest. But most of all, I bless you with knowing how much you are loved by your heavenly Father and that He is always fighting for you and the promises He gives you! He will be faithful to see you through to completion!

—MINDY RIVAS

Your Wedding Song

For the director of music. …A wedding song. My heart is stirred by a noble theme as I recite my verses for the king (Psalm 45:1).

COMMENT

Psalm 45 is not just one more wedding song. This song is for the wedding of the king. And not just any king, but King Jesus and His Bride.

No, the Old Testament psalm doesn't mention Jesus by name. But Hebrews 1:8 confirms that this song is for Him. The author of Hebrews says, "*But about the Son he* [God] *says, 'Your throne, O God, will last for ever and ever; a scepter of justice will be the scepter of your kingdom'*"—a word-for-word quote from Psalm 45:6.

So who is this King's Bride? Please believe that the King's beloved is you! This psalm is the eternal wedding song between you and your Bridegroom King.

"Let the king be enthralled by your beauty," the psalmist urges in verse 11. Note that nothing in this wedding song talks about work the bride is to do. The King has servants aplenty for that sort of thing. Rather, the bride's job is to be robed in beauty and led into the King's presence so He can be enthralled with the bride's beauty. Then the bride can transfer affection and ties from earthly attachments to the Bridegroom King.

NEXT STEPS

1. Download "Wedding Song" by David Brymer. Close your eyes and soak in this song based on Psalm 45.

2. Read slowly and savor all of Psalm 45. Read what your Bridegroom King is like (verses 1-8). Read what the bride of our Bridegroom King is like (verses 9-15). Meditate on who He is and who you are.

3. If you haven't done so, start a journal with the Lord. Write down what He thinks about His bride and what He wants His bride to do.

4. Spend time alone with the Lord, and let the King tell you how beautiful you are.

BLESSING

I bless you to sing the song of the bride, to let the King be enthralled by your beauty.

—GARLAND COHEN

WALTZING WITH THE ONE WHO LOVES ME

---------- SCRIPTURE ----------

You alone created my inner being. You knitted me together inside my mother. I will give thanks to you because I have been so amazingly and miraculously made. Your works are miraculous, and my soul is fully aware of this (Psalm 139:13-14 GW).

---------- COMMENT ----------

I had come to the ballroom dance just to shut the mouths—at least for a while—of family and friends who believed I was turning into a hermit. At least that was what I hoped to do. But I didn't really want to be there. I simply was not interested in being around people.

I was in a "poor me" phase—and, I might add, quite satisfied with feeling sorry for myself.

Unlike so many of my friends, I was not hearing Him or feeling Him close to me. Nor did I get much from reading about Him or what He said in the Bible.

But I longed for intimacy with Jesus. More than anything else, I wanted to see His face, hear His voice, and feel His presence!

Was something wrong with my eyes, ears, and sense of touch? What does a person have to do? Or had I done something that made Him turn His back to me? Was I not good enough? Maybe I just wasn't worthy of intimacy. Why the disconnect? Had I erected an impenetrable something between Jesus and me?

Yet, there I was, in the middle of an elegant ballroom, wearing a gown that others insisted I wear. They dug through to the back of my closet and pulled out my white ball gown. Shimmering white and trimmed in red and gold, it was even more beautiful than I remembered. Seeing it triggered memories of when I received it and who had given it to me.

The orchestra was beginning to play a waltz, and I was being escorted to the floor to join the other guests. I had accepted my partner's offer without looking to see who He was. As we danced, I noticed that He was a *really* good dancer. I began to relax and allow Him to lead. At some point, I was caught up with the music and decided to engage in this dance with Him. My body was responding to His gentle signals to move either to the right or left, or to turn, or to pause.

Wow! There was strength in His arms and a sureness in His step. He was certainly one of the best dance partners I'd ever had. I thought I could easily learn to trust this dance partner.

I decided to look at my partner the next time He would prepare me for a turn. Here we go! Oh my! His face, those eyes—and what they were saying to me.

His features were strong, but His look was gentle. His eyes were full of compassion and understanding. They were fixed upon me, waiting patiently for me to notice Him. As I gazed within, I saw more—a tenderness and love, so pure and accepting. It left me breathless.

He smiled as He watched my reaction to His love for me. His eyes never wandered from my face. I seemed to be all that mattered to Him. Now I understood the song, "I Only Have Eyes for You"!

I felt so special that I almost felt sorry that the other attendees were not experiencing my joy. I glanced around the room to check them out.

I gasped. Every couple seemed to be as enraptured with one another as we were. Upon a closer look, I saw that every male dance partner was the same as mine. It was Jesus! And in each case, He only had eyes for the one He was dancing with.

There was no need for comparison, jealousy, or worth-lessness. His focused love and delight were for each of us with our unique talents, skills, and gifting. After all, He made us and took great pleasure when He looked at us.

I found myself thinking that I often evaluate myself and realize that I am believing lies that have been stra-tegically placed upon me by our enemy. Was I ready to acknowledge my sin and cast off this heavy coat of decep-tion and decide to keep the white robe on?

NEXT STEPS

1. If the white robe is the righteousness that Jesus clothes us in, are you wearing that robe in your daily life? If it's not on you, what made you stop wearing it? What are you wearing in its place?

2. What lies have stopped up your ears from hearing your beloved dance partner? Are you wearing any glasses or contacts with gray-colored lenses that only see criticism and rejection?

3. Have you shielded your heart from the One who wants to love and guide you? This week, spend time with Jesus and let Him love you and guide your life. You might even ask Him about the dance He wants to lead you in. For example, you can ask Him how He's leading you and how to respond to His leading.

BLESSING

Lord, thank You for the time and pleasure You took when forming me. I am who You made me to be, Your masterpiece! Open my eyes to see Your truth and touch my heart to believe and receive it.

I bless you, in Jesus' name, to wear the white robe of righteousness and know that God has given you His righteousness. There is no room for guilt or shame in the intimacy of the dance with your Beloved. May you see His face and hear His gentle voice and so fall more in love with Him. Amen.

—SHERYL BEACON

GOING WHERE GOD IS

We have confidence to enter the Most Holy Place by the blood of Jesus, by a new and living way opened for us through the curtain, that is, his body, and since we have a great priest over the house of God, let us draw near to God with a sincere heart and with the full assurance that faith brings (Hebrews 10:19-22).

COMMENT

Before Jesus' sacrifice, access to God was, to say the least, limited. God resided in the Most Holy Place, or the Holy of Holies, within the tabernacle. But the only person who was allowed to be in there with God was the high priest. And he could only go in once a year on Yom Kippur, the Day of Atonement, when he would offer the blood of a spotless lamb for the people's sins.

No one else was allowed in the Holy of Holies, because a sinful person coming into the presence of a holy God meant instant death. In fact, the Jews would tie a rope around the high priest's leg when he went in the Holy of Holies so that if he had sinned and was killed he could be dragged out. Otherwise, the dead man would just stay in the Most Holy Place because anyone else going in would die.

But under the New Covenant, I am invited into the Holy of Holies, where God is. And I can go in just as I am, because Jesus' sacrifice has made me righteous. Sin can no longer separate me from God, who proclaims instead that He doesn't even remember my sins! (See Hebrews 10:17.)

So because I'm now a saint and not a sinner, I have a completely open access into God's throne room. Do you know the famous picture of President John F. Kennedy's son playing in the desk while his father worked (taken by photojournalist Stanley Tretick)?

His dad was the most powerful man in the world. But to his son, he was just Daddy who would always let him play in his office.

I think God and I are like this. I can go into the Most Holy Place whenever I want and have fun being with my Daddy, even though He is God.

NEXT STEPS

In your time with the Father this week, you might sit quietly with your Father and listen as you ask Him the following questions:

1. What is something You like about me?

2. What is something about Your love that I don't know yet?

3. What new thing do You want to tell or show me?

BLESSING

I bless you this week with intimacy and joy as you spend time with your Daddy in the Most Holy Place. Let it be. Amen and amen.

—RHOLAN WONG

About Rholan Wong

Rholan Wong is the Dean of Students at Kingdom Space Los Angeles, a ministry based on Bethel Church's School of Supernatural Ministry.

He previously was a student in the inaugural class of the Southern California School of Supernatural Ministry in 2012 and subsequently joined the school's staff.

He has earned a B.A. and M.A. in English Literature and published in several local and national publications. He lives in West Los Angeles with his wife Debbie. They have two adult married children, Derek and Rianna.